THE CHOSEN ONE(s)
a play about destiny(s)

by David Andrew Laws

Uproar Theatrics

**LICENSING &
PRODUCTION INQUIRIES
Uproar Theatrics, LLC.
hello@uproartheatrics.com | www.UproarTheatrics.com**

The Chosen One(s)
© 2025 David Andrew Laws

The Chosen One(s) is published by Uproar Theatrics, LLC
500 8th Ave FRNT 3, #1714 New York, NY 10018

ISBN: 978-1-968051-41-9

First Printing, January 2026

CHARACTERS

<u>The Powers That Be</u>
The Warden of The Past (PTB 1)
The Warden of The Present (PTB 2)
The Warden of That Which Is Yet to Come into Being but One Day Will (PTB 3)

<u>The Chosen One(s)</u>
The BOY WIZARD – an annoying and magical character legally distinct from Harry Potter
The BROODING HACKER – Neo meets John Nada meets Batman
The ASS-KICKING TEEN – Buffy Anne Summers meets Juliet Starling meets Rey Skywalker
The SILENT PROTAGONIST – Link meets The Courier meets Gordon Freeman
The RELUCTANT BLOND – Luke Skywalker meets Bruce Banner meets Frodo Baggins
The BRAVE VOLUNTEER – Katniss Everdeen meets Ellie Williams meets Wonder Woman
The SON OF THE GODS – Percy Jackson meets Hercules meets Thor

<u>The Antagonists</u>
The LANDLORD – a scumbag with the energy of Big Mean Carl from The Muppets
The FANATIC – an obsessive creature with the energy of Gollum from The Lord of The Rings
The OVERTHINKER – a villainous force of destruction
The GRUNTS – nameless, indistinguishable cannon fodder
The RAVENOUS MAW – a monster in The OVERTHINKER's employ
The TOXIC TRIAD SISTERS – The OVERTHINKER's villainous trio of warriors
JEFF – a guy The OVERTHINKER paid twenty bucks to get in The Chosen Ones' way

<u>The Others</u>
The CUSTOMER – a customer and proud nerd
The MENTOR – Gandalf meets Obi Wan meets Merlin
The GOD FATHER – Zeus, one of The SON OF THE GODS' dads
POSEIDON – the voice of one of The SON OF THE GODS' other dads
The VENDOR – a vendor in the park selling magical goods
VOICE – an announcer-ly tool of exposition and mood-setting

A Note on Casting – Diversity is good! Casting should reflect the talents and types in the room, not any preconceptions about race or gender that any of these roles might project. Characters should use and respect one another's stated pronouns, but can be played by anyone.

Other Notes –

- *sigh* <u>Yes</u>, the character of "The Ass-Kicking Teen" *can* be represented as "The Butt-Kicking Teen" where needed. It's not a <u>good</u> choice, but it's an available adjustment if wooing a prudish board member is the only way to get the show produced. In that vein, all instances of "ass" can be changed to butt for the aforementioned reason.
- Specificity of staging in this piece is, for the most part, a guideline. Lines, on the other hand, are very strictly structured: moments when characters have individualized lines are always important (except the ones that are for throwing away) and moments when characters speak simultaneously should be jumbled and indecipherable. There is even room for some ab libbing in these moments, as long as they maintain the spirit of the text.
- This show is all about pacing. It is the intersection of the traditional hero's journey cycle matched with the presentational energy of *The Play That Goes Wrong*. To an extent, all of the characters know they're characters presenting a story, and that impacts the way they interact with both the narrative and the audience, whether that's to try to lean into getting audience attention/reaction or fervently ignoring them and attempting to give an award-winning performance from behind their own fourth wall. In either case, everything is very real, and nothing should be pretended except for what is pretend.
- Dialogue in **bold** indicates emphasis by volume. <u>Underlined</u> dialogue indicates emphasis by tempo. The "//" symbol indicates an overlap in dialogue between characters or actions.

Special Thanks to Isabella Greathouse, Giselle Muise, Sophia Carlin, Daniel Morrison, Michele Danna, Zaramaria Fas, Allison Wein, Maera Hagage, Lee (Emry) Sottile, Darcy Thompson, Gregory Petershack, Kyle Holmes, Laura Hall, and, ever and always, Alexandra Abney

PROLOGUE

A liminal space.

The stage is dark and blank. The curtain is down, if applicable. The air of awe and mystery is amplified by the technical design: a low rumble in the soundscape, a twinkling of lights, perhaps a light rolling fog – whatever can be done to foster an atmosphere of intrigue and oncoming adventure.

A VOICE speaks from the darkness.

VOICE

Before there was life, there was…The Prophecy! And The Prophecy foretold evil. And The Prophecy foretold good. And The Prophecy foretold that a hero would rise so that a villain could fall. The Prophecy foretold a great journey: of reluctance and change, of thresholds and mentors, of trials and transformations, of death and rebirth. And at the center of it all, The Prophecy foretold…a chosen one!!

(The curtain rises, or the theatrical equivalent occurs. Booming, eventful music. A clap of thunder? The stage is still blank, but we see shapes in the mist. Assembled in the darkness are The BOY WIZARD, The BROODING HACKER, The RELUCTANT BLOND, The SILENT PROTAGONIST, The ASS-KICKING TEEN, The BRAVE VOLUNTEER, and The SON OF THE GODS arranged in a frozen tableau that will look totally super epic and cool once it is revealed. Each of them is striking their own character-defining pose, but the sum of their poses is even more awesome than their parts. We just can't see it yet.

1

*PTB 1 enters SL, moving DSR as they speak. He
is impressive and imposing, lit either by a
spotlight or a handheld light.)*

PTB 1

(with a rich and put-on presentational voice) What **makes** a
hero? Are they born? Created? Or sprung from something…
other?

*(PTB 2 enters SR, moving to join PTB 1 DSR as
she speaks. She is graceful and powerful, and lit
in the same way as PTB 1.)*

PTB 2

*(with an equally-rich and equally-put-on presentational
voice)* What **is** destiny? Is it with us from birth? Or do the
steps of our lives determine our path?

(PTB 3 enters DSL. They are…not lit.)

PTB 3

*(trying to be grand and presentational, but not as practiced
at it as the other two)* How **did**…you guys…get your lights
to come on?

*(PTB 3 tries, in the darkness, to get their light to
come on, waving at the back of the house,
clapping their hands, snapping their fingers if
trying to summon a spotlight or whacking the
lighting tool if it's something handheld. PTB 1
watches with disdain. PTB 2 watches with
concern. Eventually, not because of anything
PTB 3 did, ideally even in a moment when
they've given up, their light comes on.)*

PTB 3

(very natural, almost mumbled under their breath) …ah, there we go. Okay.

(PTB 1 tries to revive some of the grandeur.)

PTB 1

(a grand presentation once more) The tapestry that displays the story of life is vast and complex,

PTB 2

(oozing with intrigue) Weaved together by unseen, unheard, and unknown forces from beyond,

PTB 3

(trying their best) **That's us**.

(The Powers That Be introduce themselves with the utmost formality.)

PTB 1

I, The Warden of The Past,

PTB 2

I, The Warden of The Present,

PTB 3

And I, The Warden of That Which Is Yet to Come into Being but One Day Will.

PTB 1

We–… *(glaring over at PTB 3)* "The Future." Just call yourself "The Warden of the Future."

PTB 3

…you guys are so much better at this than I am.

PTB 1

But, though we are mighty, we may not interfere,

PTB 2

Our efforts must be used to guide and to steer,

(PTB 3 doesn't chime in. PTB 1 and PTB 2 look at PTB 3 expectantly. After a moment, PTB 3 realizes but doesn't know what to say.)

PTB 3

(trying their best) Mm-hm.

PTB 1

(plowing through) For our presence is too mighty, our power too great,

PTB 2

Which is why we serve as the puppeteers of fate,

PTB 3

Oh, I get it, we're rhyming, and I realized too late.

PTB 1

Now the world needs saving from evil and wrong,

PTB 2

A hero remembered through story and song,

PTB 3

(with a swing of their leg) Someone to kick villains right in the dong.

PTB 1

That is why we, the Powers That Be,

PTB 2

We, the all-seeing three,

PTB 3

We…the…ones who…<u>are</u> <u>we</u>,

PTB ALL

We have elected…**a chosen one**!

(The Powers That Be gesture toward the group of Chosen Ones in the dark)

PTB ALL

Prepare for your hero…

PTB 1. *(simultaneous)* The Silent Protagonist!
PTB 2. *(simultaneous)* The Son of the Gods!
PTB 3. *(simultaneous)* The Reluctant Blond!

(A light or lights come[s] up on The SILENT PROTAGONIST, The SON OF THE GODS, and The RELUCTANT BLOND, each striking their heroic pose. Some of the light bleeds onto the ones who weren't named.)

PTB 1

Wait, what?

(The Powers That Be look between themselves and The Chosen Ones with confusion. The Chosen Ones aren't sure what to do with themselves. Some of them are better at hiding their confusion and concern, but they all keep it together more or less, just a few furtive glances here and there.)

5

PTB 2

Why would you choose a **silent** protagonist? How's he gonna do any quippy dialogue?

PTB 1

At least **my** Chosen One will have some obstacles to overcome – "Son of the Gods?" Talk about a nepo baby.

PTB 3

Yeah, and why'd I get stuck with The Reluctant Blond? What, he's blond and doesn't wanna be here?

PTB 1

What? No one made– YOU chose your chosen one!!

PTB 2

(genuinely curious) And what does him being blond have to do with his archetype?

PTB 3

I DON'T KNOW!

PTB 1

(with a double-handed 'zip it' gesture) Alright. We were all <u>supposed</u> to pick the same one. That's kind of the point of having a chosen ONE?

PTB 3

(observing the group) Maybe some of them are a red herring…?

PTB 2

Ooh, or a double bluff!

PTB 3

OOH, or a deus ex machina!

PTB 1

Stop it, now you're both just naming tropes. *(pushing forward)* Let's see who we're working with.

(PTB 1 waves his hand and the lights come up on the full cadre of Chosen Ones.)

PTB 3

(looking around, impressed at how easily PTB 1 turned on the lights; so naturalistic the line might actually be missed) Ah, nice.

(The fuller light allows some of The Chosen Ones to relax a little, while being seen but uncalled makes others tense up more. PTB 1 mentally tallies The Chosen Ones, then turns back to PTB 2 and PTB 3.)

PTB 1

Seven?? Between the three of us, we elected <u>seven</u> avatars of destiny?

PTB 2

I didn't know we had to be unanimous, so I had one and a back-up in case the first one beefed it.

PTB 3

Me too. That or, you know, sequel bait.

PTB 1

(considering) Huh, that's kinda what I did too. *(snapping out of it)* But no! There's got to be **one** Chosen One, so let's... <u>choose</u>. One.

PTB 2

But which one?

PTB 1

Well, we've got options. Let's see who we're playing with. I
had…

*(The Powers That Be turn back to the group of
Chosen Ones.)*

PTB 1

(back in presenting voice) **The Silent Protagonist**!

*(The SILENT PROTAGONIST steps forward.
More likely does a big kick jump forward and
makes a video-game-like effort noise.)*

SILENT PROTAGONIST

Hyyyah!

PTB 2

Not exactly silent.

PTB 1

He's not **mute**; he just doesn't **speak**. Makes him easier to
connect with. Audiences look at The Silent Protagonist and
go "That? That's me."

*(The Powers That Be look out at the audience,
then back at The SILENT PROTAGONIST and
how silly he's dressed.)*

PTB 1

Well, *(looks back at the audience)* some audiences. *(looks
back at the group of Chosen Ones)* And if he didn't test well,
I was going to offer up… *(presenting)* **The Brave
Volunteer**!

*(The BRAVE VOLUNTEER moves forward,
notches an arrow, and fires it offstage.)*

BRAVE VOLUNTEER
I'll do whatever it takes to protect my home and the family I
love.

PTB 3
What's so special about <u>her</u>? They're <u>all</u> brave. They're
answering the summons of a life-changing quest.

PTB 1
(confident throughout) Yes, but this one's *(reaching)* …a
volunteer.

PTB 2
So she's not going to refuse the call to adventure?

PTB 1
I mean, she <u>is</u>, but then, she'll, like…volunteer to…– Shut
up! Alright? Show me yours if you're so smart.

PTB 2
Gladly. My carefully crafted main character is…*(presenting)*
The Son of the Gods!

> *(The SON OF THE GODS slides into position
> with the crash of a wave and a crack of
> lightning.)*

SON OF THE GODS
With the power of the heavens on my side, nothing will
stand in my way!

> *(PTB 1 and PTB 3 are unimpressed. PTB 1
> makes a fart noise with his mouth.)*

PTB 3
That kid is, like, twelve.

PTB 2

He's seventeen!

PTB 1

And he seems <u>way</u> overpowered. What's his backstory?

PTB 2

(defensively) He's the son of Zeus! *(bashfully)* And
Poseidon. *(rattling them off)* And Hades and Athena and
Ares and Dionysus and Aphrodite from an alternate universe
where they could all have a son together without it being
weird.

PTB 1

Bit of a stretch.

PTB 2

Well, just in case, I was also prepared to offer up...
(presenting) **The Ass-Kicking Teen**.

> *(The ASS-KICKING TEEN takes CS with a
> roundoff or other gymnastic feat.)*

ASS-KICKING TEEN

Vampires? Zombies? I'm more scared of failing my
geometry midterm.

PTB 1

(impressed) That's some real final-girl energy.

PTB 2

(excited) And then, in a best-case scenario, Ass-Kicking
Teen and The Son of the Gods have this "will-they, won't-
they" chemistry that allows for a <u>very</u> engaging spin-off
series, if you know what I mean.

PTB 1

Alright, alright, now is not the time for fan fiction.

PTB 2
There's <u>always</u> time for fan fiction.

PTB 3
(wiggling their eyebrows) I like it.

PTB 1
(to PTB 3) Keep it in your prologue. Who'd you choose?

PTB 3
(clearing their throat) I chose...apparently...**The Reluctant Blond**!

> *(The RELUCTANT BLOND steps into position with a slouch and a lot of hidden potential.)*

RELUCTANT BLOND
(whiny) But I was going into Smoshi Station to pick up some capacity transformers.

PTB 2
Whiny.

PTB 1
And blond. *(with the sub-text of 'remind me')* Why is that important?

PTB 3
I don't know!!!

PTB 2
Does he have powers or...?

PTB 3

(self-conscious) Yeah…but they're, like, really under the surface, and they keep getting retconned and contextualized and…forget it, whatever. I've <u>also</u> got…*(thinking; remembering)* oh, *(presenting)* **The Brooding Hacker**.

(The BROODING HACKER steps forward, speaking through or overtop of outrageously-dark sunglasses.)

BROODING HACKER

I'm here to hack computers and alter realities, and I'm all outta computers.

(PTB 1 and PTB 2 look back at PTB 3.)

PTB 3

Yeah, I gotta admit, in a group project, I usually let you guys do all the heavy lifting.

PTB 2

I'll say.

PTB 1

But wait, that's everyone accounted for: *(pointing two fingers at PTB 2)* yours, *(two fingers at PTB 3)* and yours, *(two fingers at themself)* and mine. *(at The BOY WIZARD)* Then who's that?

(The BOY WIZARD moves DS of all of the other Chosen Ones.)

BOY WIZARD

(with too much energy) I AM THE BOY WIZARD! I'M HERE TO STOP EVIL AND SAVE THE DAY USING MAGIC AND THE POWER OF FRIENDSHIP!

(The Powers That Be simultaneously jeer at The BOY WIZARD, chasing him off with their vitriol. Suggested lines are below, but they really lay into him, growing in intensity until he exits.)

PTB 1 *(simultaneous)* Oh my god, no, it's not about you. Learn to interpret ancient lore, you little–. Get outta here! We hate you!!

PTB 2. *(simultaneous)* Not this guy again. Gimmie a break. You don't even use your magic consistently. Scram, you little power creep!!

PTB 3. *(simultaneous)* No no no, I'm gonna break your wand in half and throw both bits into two different volcanoes if you don't get lost, you **loser**!!

(Once The BOY WIZARD leaves, The Powers That Be compose themselves.)

PTB 1
(to the audience) Sorry about that. *(back to the group)* So.

PTB 2
So.

PTB 3
I really hate that guy.

PTB 1
(quickly) I know, I know, I know. *(taking control)* But. We've got a world to save.

PTB 2
Well... *(of The Chosen Ones)* one of them does.

PTB 3
But which one?

                          PTB 1
Yyyyeah...they're all relatively-compelling protagonists.

                          PTB 3
(stalling until they have an idea) Iiiiiiiiiiiiiiiiii have an idea.

                          PTB 1
Do tell.

                          PTB 3
It's slightly unorthodox, but. What if we...go... *(shrugs their shoulders and makes a little noise)* 'hm?'

                    (There is a moment where PTB1 & PTB2 just look at PTB3.)

                          PTB 1
(shrugging his shoulders and making a little noise to confirm) 'Hm?'

                          PTB 2
(testing out the movement and the noise as well) 'Hm.' I mean...

                          PTB 1
You want us to leave the balance of good and evil in the universe up to 'hm??'

                          PTB 3
No! *(of The Chosen Ones)* I want us to leave it up to one of them, but like, isn't that the whole point of a grand, unknowable prediction? Sometimes no one knows who "The Chosen One" is until everybody's neck-deep in the denouement. Maybe we just infuse all six of them with a lot of potential and...hope for the best.

PTB 2
(reminding PTB 1; shrugging) 'Hm.'

PTB 3
(agreeing; shrugging) 'Hm.'

PTB 1
(looking back at The Chosen Ones; contemplating) It <u>would</u> increase the odds of <u>my</u> Chosen One being the one that saves the day.

PTB 2
(suddenly excited) I'll take that bet. Loser has to spend a week in the Time Shredder?

PTB 1
(shaking PTB 2's hand) You're on.

PTB 3
Aw, I didn't…. *(acquiescing)* Alright. *(to the audience; shrugging)* 'Hm.'

> *(PTB 1 turns back to the audience, leading the charge back into the presentational.)*

PTB 1
(presenting) Prepare for a story only time can tell,

PTB 2
(presenting) On a journey new, though known quite well.

PTB 3
(presenting as best they can) Aaaand we're rhyming again, isn't that swell?

PTB 1
Which heroes will rise, and which ones will fall?

PTB 2
Which plotlines will falter and which will stand tall?

PTB 3
Act wisely, Chosen Ones. We're counting on y'all.

PTB 1
Heroes. We grant you your potential. But your destinies are yours to fulfill. And your journey begins...

PTB ALL

NOW!

(The lights and sound rise into a tremendous din before crashing into a BLACKOUT!)

> *The Brooding Hacker's apartment.*

> *The Brooding Hacker's apartment is a mess. A big, blocky computer monitor, a keyboard, and a computer mouse sit on a desk. The computer is surrounded, but not covered, by debris. The BROODING HACKER is asleep on the couch, one arm laid stoically over his eyes. The door, or more thematically the suggestion of a door, is SL. There is a knock at the door.*

BROODING HACKER
(without moving) Go away.

> *(A pause and then a more insistent knock)*

BROODING HACKER
I said, 'Go away.'

> *(A pause and then a third knock. The BROODING HACKER rises from the couch and opens {or "opens"} the door in one fluid motion.)*

BROODING HACKER
What part of—

> *(He is interrupted by The ASS-KICKING TEEN who enters SL, pizza box in hand, and moves past him via an impressive gymnastic stunt. She lands near the middle of the room and gives him a thumbs-up that turns into a finger pointing at him.)*

ASS-KICKING TEEN
(snarkily) Listen, dude. <u>You're</u> the one who ordered the pizza.

BROODING HACKER
(searching in his pockets for cash) Oh…yeah, I guess I did. How much do I owe you?

ASS-KICKING TEEN
That'll be twenty-seven fifty.

(The BROODING HACKER freezes mid-search.)

BROODING HACKER
(with grave import) Wait!

(The ASS-KICKING TEEN freezes.)

BROODING HACKER
(narrowing his eyes) Say that again….

ASS-KICKING TEEN
That'll be twenty-seven fifty, weirdo.

BROODING HACKER
That's it!

(The BROODING HACKER rushes over to the computer, brushing things off the desk frantically, even though doing so doesn't give him any better access to the keyboard.)

BROODING HACKER
(typing wildly as he speaks) Twenty-seven fifty, aka two-thousand, seven-hundred and fifty. The product of a small prime, a cube, and a square, this number has sixteen divisors. <u>Sixteen.</u> Sixteen main-belt asteroids broke free of their orbits

BROODING HACKER (CONT)
sixteen years ago and <u>one</u> of them has been hurtling toward
earth ever since.

*(The ASS-KICKING TEEN joins The
BROODING HACKER at the computer,
bumping him a little to the side with her hip so
that she can type beside him with her free hand.)*

ASS-KICKING TEEN
Twenty-seven fifty <u>also</u> translates in a hexadecimal cipher to
the letters A, B, E, or "Abe". Abe Lincoln was the sixteenth
president of the United States, and his birthplace was in
Larue County, Kentucky.

BROODING HACKER
(typing alongside her) So if we triangulate the asteroid's
trajectory with that location in mind–

ASS-KICKING TEEN
–we can calculate the precise moment of impact, the size of
the impending tremors–

BROODING HACKER
–and the exact moment I need to power up my time machine
in order to ride the wave of kinetic energy and open a portal
to the future.

ASS-KICKING TEEN
(stepping away from the computer) Time machine?? Whoa
whoa whoa, who said anything about a portal to the future,
pal?

BROODING HACKER
(pointing to himself with a thumb at his chest) I did. *(back to
the computer, typing frenetically)* To the year 2750, to be
exact, when the second singularity will give robots

BROODING HACKER (CONT)
reproductive rights and humanity's usefulness will finally
come to an end. *(like a badass)* Unless, that is, somebody
goes forward in time and stops it.

> *(The BROODING HACKER rears up his arm
> and does a final big button press on the
> keyboard.)*

BROODING HACKER
(with enormous satisfaction) **There**.

> *(The BROODING HACKER and The ASS-
> KICKING TEEN both stare at the screen in
> wonder.)*

BROODING HACKER
The shockwave should hit us in exactly twenty-seven
minutes and fifty seconds.

ASS-KICKING TEEN
Wow.

BROODING HACKER
Think that's enough time to finish a large pepperoni with
extra onions?

ASS-KICKING TEEN
(checking the receipt on the pizza box) Oh, did you get extra
onions?

BROODING HACKER
(folding his arms and leaning against the desk) I always do.

ASS-KICKING TEEN
Oh, my bad. Then the actual total is thirty-two twelve.

20

BROODING HACKER

Oh. *(thinks for a moment, then knocks the computer off the desk {ideally with an exaggerated crash})* Never mind. Let me try to find some cash.

> *(The BROODING HACKER starts searching around the room, in the debris, under the couch cushions, as the conversation continues.)*

ASS-KICKING TEEN

(observing the mess) Sooo, do you always live like this, or…?

BROODING HACKER

I'm a bit of a loner.

ASS-KICKING TEEN

Yeah, so's the kid in my AP Calc class who might be a werewolf.

BROODING HACKER

(stopping momentarily to observe her) You live a weird life, don't you?

ASS-KICKING TEEN

Oh, I wouldn't say that. Don't get me wrong, I've got a best friend who's a witch and a best friend whose soul is stuck in a vacuum cleaner, and we solve mysteries around the school with the help of a janitor with glowing green eyes. But at the end of the day, I'm just your average teenage girl hoping to find a date to prom.

BROODING HACKER

(snarkily; going back to searching for cash) I'm a little old for prom.

ASS-KICKING TEEN
Ew. You're a little too a lotta things for prom. *(looking around)* Should I help you look or something? Your pizza's gonna get cold.

BROODING HACKER
(with grave import) Wait…say that again.

(There is an interrupting knock at the door. The BROODING HACKER crosses to it.)

ASS-KICKING TEEN
My my, you're pretty popular for a loner.

BROODING HACKER
(with smarm) I always am.

(The BROODING HACKER "opens" {or opens} the door and The LANDLORD, Mr. Neece, enters.)

MR. NEECE
Hey, you! Where's my rent money??

BROODING HACKER
(a little intimidated) Mr. Nice. Neece to see you.

MR. NEECE
No, it's **not**. It's Mr. **Neece** and it's **nice** to see me. And no it's **not** cause I'm angry cause where's my rent money??

BROODING HACKER
Well…I don't exactly have it.

ASS-KICKING TEEN
Heh. So I guess this means no tip?

MR. NEECE

(to The ASS-KICKING TEEN) And you! Don't you live upstairs in apartment thirty-two twelve?

ASS-KICKING TEEN

(looking around the apartment) I thought this place looked familiar. *(to The LANDLORD)* Maybe I do. Who's askin'?

MR. NEECE

Me! Your landlord. Where's my rent money?

ASS-KICKING TEEN

What're you askin' **me** for? I'm a teenager!

MR. NEECE

Well then I guess you shouldn't have taken out a two-year lease on a studio apartment!

ASS-KICKING TEEN

Well then I guess <u>you</u> shouldn't have trusted a high school senior with such a massive financial decision.

MR. NEECE

Well then I guess **<u>you</u>** shouldn't have been a legally-emancipated minor who passed a credit check and successfully provided a friendly local janitor as a guarantor!

ASS-KICKING TEEN

…yeah, okay, that's on me. He <u>is</u> a ghost now….

MR. NEECE

Now gimmie my rent money, or get out, **both** of ya!

BROODING HACKER

Let's all calm down here. There's got to be a way to settle this.

MR. NEECE

No no no, you're not gonna talk your way outta this one.
Because it's not just about the rent with you two. *(to The
ASS-KICKING TEEN)* Every time you conduct a seance in
your living room or find an ancient cursed artifact at the
local grocery store, my property values drop like a rock. *(to
The BROODING HACKER)* And you! Typing like a
madman and monologuing to yourself at all hours. None of
us can get any **sleep**!

ASS-KICKING TEEN

You really are a loner, huh?

BROODING HACKER

(snarkily) I always am.

LANDLORD

(with the subtext 'ugh') And the **banter**! If I hear one more
snarky quip out of either of you, I'll not only kick you out,
I'll ban you from renting in this neighborhood ever again!

BROODING HACKER

(an outburst) Wait!

> *(There is a pause where we think he might
> actually say something important or even
> relevant. But then...)*

BROODING HACKER

(with the gravest import yet) ...say that again.

> *(Blackout! with the sound of power shutting
> down or a big door slam.)*

ACT I, SCENE II

A nearby park.

The transition from apartment to park is swift and efficient. The couch and desk go away and a park bench is brought CS. Or maybe the couch becomes a park bench, it's your design process. A few bushes dot the landscape. Maybe a tree. The debris and even the computer monitor can stay; it's not a very nice park.

The BROODING HACKER and The ASS-KICKING TEEN sit despondently on the bench, sharing the pizza from before.

ASS-KICKING TEEN

Extra onions was a dastardly call. *(tapping her chest with her fist in discomfort)* Aren't you worried about heartburn?

BROODING HACKER

(dejected but still brooding) I always am.

ASS-KICKING TEEN

That one didn't really work....

BROODING HACKER

I **know**, okay?? It's a defense mechanism, get off my back!

ASS-KICKING TEEN

Alright! Alright. *(beat)* I can't believe we actually aren't allowed to rent in this neighborhood again.

BROODING HACKER

(doesn't want to think about it) Yeah.

ASS-KICKING TEEN
Like, I thought he was being hyperbolic, like, 'how does he even have the power to do that?', but I guess he does.

BROODING HACKER
(head in his hands; really doesn't want to think about it)
YEAH.

ASS-KICKING TEEN
(in an attempt to change the subject) Sorry I messed up your calculations.

BROODING HACKER
Eh, it's okay. Maybe the asteroid'll miss us entirely. Maybe the robot uprising won't even happen. Maybe I'll never get to save the world from a cataclysmic event.

ASS-KICKING TEEN
And that's a bad thing?

BROODING HACKER
I just… *(with a hefty sigh; standing and gazing out into the middle distance)* All my life, I've felt like I was destined for greatness. Like someday I'd be thrust into a situation where only I could save the day.

ASS-KICKING TEEN
Save the day from what?

BROODING HACKER
Anything. An alien invasion. Corrupt A.I. overlords. Whatever it took to prove that I wasn't just special…I was really special.

ASS-KICKING TEEN
The gifted student burnout is real.

BROODING HACKER

Instead it's, wake up, do my job, deep dive about conspiracy theories for an hour or two on company time, go home, not save the world, go to bed. The world never seems to need saving in a way that I can save it. That asteroid thing turned out to be a total bust; AI's not dangerous yet, it's just good at chess and bad at poetry; one time I thought maybe aliens were using my body as a battery, but it turns out I just had an iron deficiency.

ASS-KICKING TEEN

Hey, I get it. It feels like every week there's an anomaly in the gymnasium or the A/V Club's getting possessed by a demon. I wrap it up in a succinct little easy-to-digest storyline, and everyone learns a handy-dandy life lesson along the way, but…it gets monotonous. Just once I'd like to be faced with a paradigm-shifting, life-defining series of events that puts my true character to the test. Maybe then I could put my nunchucks away for good and finally be… normal.

BROODING HACKER

(wryly) We really are quite a pair, aren't we?

ASS-KICKING TEEN

(with a chuckle) A pair of what?

BROODING HACKER

A pair of loners?

ASS-KICKING TEEN

More like a pair of losers.

(The BOY WIZARD pops out from behind a tree or, if there's no tree, out of a bush, or if there's no bushes or trees, from offstage right.)

BOY WIZARD
(far too enthusiastically) Maybe **I** can help!

> *(The ASS-KICKING TEEN leaps into a battle stance.)*

ASS-KICKING TEEN
Waaagh!

> *(The BROODING HACKER groans and puts his head back in his hands.)*

BROODING HACKER
Not now....

BOY WIZARD
I can help you get your apartments back and get your lives back on track! With <u>magic</u>! And the power of <u>friendship</u>.

BROODING HACKER
(to The ASS-KICKING TEEN) Just ignore him.

ASS-KICKING TEEN
You know this guy?

BROODING HACKER
Everybody knows this guy. *(to The BOY WIZARD)* Shouldn't you be at your fancy boarding school across the pond?

BOY WIZARD
(a little ashamed) We had to take a mid-semester break early because a poltergeist clogged all the toilets.

ASS-KICKING TEEN
Okay, well...can we help you?

BOY WIZARD

(like a mischievous little scamp) Don't you see? It is <u>I</u> who can help <u>you</u>. I can cast a spell that will take you back in time to when you <u>did</u> have money. Then you can use that money to pay for the rent that you don't have now, and your landlord will be never the wiser, mmmm!

BROODING HACKER

But then we wouldn't have the money in the **past** when we needed it **then**, and you're just creating a whole new set of problems!

ASS-KICKING TEEN

Yeah, if you've got <u>magic</u>, why wouldn't you just use it to conjure <u>money</u>? This plan seems needlessly convoluted.

BOY WIZARD

(genuinely confused) But...weren't you all talking about doing time travel earlier? How is that–?

BROODING HACKER

That was SCIENCE! That was DIFFERENT! I was going to the FUTURE! We wouldn't have even EXISTED!

BOY WIZARD

But, but if you go to the past, you could be in two places at once! Think of the whimsy!

BROODING HACKER

(threateningly) Think of the swift kick I'm gonna give you if you don't take your chronological paradoxes and get outta here!

BOY WIZARD

But–

ASS-KICKING TEEN. *(simultaneous)* I'm not gonna risk my atoms melting because you made me interact with my past self, you little wizard boy, scram, beat it!

BROODING HACKER. *(simultaneous)* You're gonna make a **time hole**! You're gonna make a **time hole** with your bad magic, get <u>outta</u> here! Get outta here, go!

BOY WIZARD
(still a little scamp) Okay, okay, no need to be such slugbears about it. *(giggling whimsily)* Mm hm hm!

(The BOY WIZARD scampers off SR.)

BROODING HACKER
That guy, I swear, he has <u>no</u> self-awareness. Always has to be the center of attention. *(with no self-awareness)* Now, where was I?

ASS-KICKING TEEN
(with irony) Brooding.

BROODING HACKER
(sits on the park bench to do just that) I always am….

> *(While The BROODING HACKER broods, The ASS-KICKING TEEN starts digging through the bushes or the debris.)*

BROODING HACKER
What are you doing?

ASS-KICKING TEEN
Seeing if the boy wizard dropped some change or something. That pizza's not gonna pay for itself.

BROODING HACKER

(sarcastically) Oh, I'm sorry! *(starts facetiously digging through his pockets)* Yeah, let's get right on that – that's <u>definitely</u> our biggest problem right now. How much was it, thirty-two twelve? Or did you forget to include sales tax, which would screw up my pointless calculations even more??

> *(The BROODING HACKER digs through one of the bushes, and The SILENT PROTAGONIST pops up, a sword in one hand and a scroll in the other.)*

SILENT PROTAGONIST

Hiiyah!

BROODING HACKER

(retreating) He's got a sword!

> *(The SILENT PROTAGONIST drops the scroll and starts hopping around the stage swinging his sword and making effort noises. Maybe he hacks at the tree. Maybe something falls out of it. Really he's just trying to figure out the controls.)*

ASS-KICKING TEEN

I'm starting to understand why my parents didn't want me to hang out at this park. *(darkly ominous)* Before they mysteriously disappeared… *(back to normal)* Do you know this guy too? Is he going to try to solve our problems by pulling a rabbit out of his ass?

BROODING HACKER

No, he seems…

> *(They watch as The SILENT PROTAGONIST tries to execute a backwards long jump, but he*

*can't quite get past the crouching and popping
back up phase. He makes little effort noises as
he tries.)*

BROODING HACKER

…harmless.

ASS-KICKING TEEN
(spotting the scroll) He dropped something.

*(The ASS-KICKING TEEN picks up the scroll
and unfurls it as she crosses.)*

ASS-KICKING TEEN
Hey, you dropped… (getting distracted by what's on the
scroll) …this….

BROODING HACKER

What is it?

*(The BROODING HACKER joins The ASS-
KICKING TEEN and reads over her shoulder. If
possible, the scroll makes their faces glow. The
SILENT PROTAGONIST watches them with
curiosity.)*

ASS-KICKING TEEN. *(simultaneous)* Whoa…
BROODING HACKER. *(simultaneous)* Whoa…

*(As the glow fades, The ASS-KICKING TEEN
stands holding the scroll contemplatively. The
BROODING HACKER taps the page with the
back of his hand and moves into his own space
to ponder.)*

BROODING HACKER

Now, that's what I'm talking about! This is exactly what we were looking for. A purpose!

                    ASS-KICKING TEEN
A calling.

                    BROODING HACKER
A legacy.

                    ASS-KICKING TEEN
A cash prize.

                    BROODING HACKER
Exactly. We do this – we'll have enough money to cover our rents and then some!

                    ASS-KICKING TEEN
In whatever neighborhood we want!

                    BROODING HACKER
(making himself stay in character) Independently though. Different neighborhoods entirely, probably, 'cause I'm a bit of a loner.

                    ASS-KICKING TEEN
(smiling) Uh huh. *(to The SILENT PROTAGONIST)* Thanks, weird...sword-wielding man in the public park.

            (The ASS-KICKING TEEN and The BROODING
            HACKER watch The SILENT PROTAGONIST
            for a moment as he explores the stage. At a
            certain point, his hit box gets caught on the edge
            of the park bench and he walks in place,
            observing the landscape around him and not
            realizing he's stuck.)

                    BROODING HACKER

Do you think he'll be alright?

ASS-KICKING TEEN
We could...bring him along? Three heads might be better than two, in this case.

BROODING HACKER
(crankily) But I'm a bit of a loner...

ASS-KICKING TEEN
(facetiously) Yeah, you mentioned. *(gesturing at the mess of a park around them)* Look where that's gotten you.

BROODING HACKER
Fair point. *(approaches The SILENT PROTAGONIST, which draws his attention; extending a hand)* What's your name, stranger?

> *(The SILENT PROTAGONIST does a backwards roll into a double jump.)*

SILENT PROTAGONIST
Hup-hah!

> *(The BROODING HACKER breathes through a moment of not understanding.)*

BROODING HACKER
Huh. Can't say it's what I'd have picked for ya, but if that's your name.

ASS-KICKING TEEN
(showing him the scroll) This is yours, right? You mind if we tag along?

SILENT PROTAGONIST
Hyyy-uh!

> *(The SILENT PROTAGONIST tosses his sword up with a flourish, catches it, then strikes a pose with a wink and a thumbs up.)*

BROODING HACKER
I'm gonna take that as a 'yes please.' Alright, then. Enough moping about. What say we get this adventure started?

> *(This sounds very appealing to The SILENT PROTAGONIST who raises his sword and rushes offstage with a cheerful yelp. The BROODING HACKER and the ASS-KICKING TEEN exchange a look and then rush off after him. There is a brief moment of transition. Then, from the opposite side of the stage, The FANATIC skulks onstage, crawling on all-fours. Perhaps a musical theme underscores his arrival. He sniffs around the park, making his way to the bench. He crouches on the park bench and picks up a slice of pizza, sniffing at it. He gazes in the direction that the other characters exited.)*

FANATIC
Yesss…we wants to go on an adventure too… *(takes a bite of pizza; clearing his throat)* <u>Ahem</u>! <u>Ahem</u>!

> *(Blackout with a big bass-y thump, either in the music or otherwise.)*

ACT I, SCENE III

A comic book shop.

*The debris from the park can go or be
assimilated into this location. The potential trees
and bushes go, as does the park bench, and on
come a counter and various racks of comic
books and other nerd paraphernalia. Not for
nothing, longboxes are a great stand-in for
seeing actual bulks of merchandise.*

*The RELUCTANT BLOND stands behind the
counter in mid-confrontation with The SON OF
THE GODS and The BRAVE VOLUNTEER. The
CUSTOMER is standing somewhere in the
background, leafing through a comic book. A
bell dings SL as The SILENT PROTAGONIST,
The ASS-KICKING TEEN, and The BROODING
HACKER jump, flip, and saunter, respectively,
into the room.*

SON OF THE GODS
(waving a scroll in The RELUCTANT BLOND'S face) What
is the meaning of this, you flaxen-headed deceiver?

RELUCTANT BLOND
(swatting at the scroll, trying to catch it) If you'll just let me
explain–...

BRAVE VOLUNTEER
(to The SON OF THE GODS) Teaming up was a mistake.
I'm getting out of here and finding someone else to save.
(gravely) Someone who really needs it....

RELUCTANT BLOND
Wait, but–!

ASS-KICKING TEEN
Is everything alright in here?

RELUCTANT BLOND
Yes, everything's fine. Welcome to– *(seeing the scroll in The ASS-KICKING TEEN'S hand)* Oh! You got my flyer too. *(with a quick survey of the room)* That puts us at a full six!

BROODING HACKER
Six what?

RELUCTANT BLOND
Adventurers!

ASS-KICKING TEEN
(striking a pose) That's right! We're here to help.

SON OF THE GODS
(to The BROODING HACKER and The ASS-KICKING TEEN) As were we, but do not fall for this charlatan's trickery.

RELUCTANT BLOND
I'm not a charlatan….

SON OF THE GODS
Then **where** is the Damsel of Lucerna Lake and what must we do to rescue her?

BROODING HACKER
Yeah, we got the call-to-arms as well. But are you sure I can't do this on my own? That's a hell of a cash prize to split six ways.

BRAVE VOLUNTEER
You <u>would</u> only be in this for the money, wouldn't you?

BROODING HACKER
Sister, you don't know anything about me.

BRAVE VOLUNTEER
(grabbing him by the lapels) How <u>dare</u> you mention my sister?

(The ASS-KICKING TEEN steps between them.)

ASS-KICKING TEEN
Alright, hands off the merchandise. We need him for now.

BROODING HACKER
Hey, I don't need anybody, so don't anybody start needing me!

ASS-KICKING TEEN
What I'm <u>saying</u> is that if blondie here says it'll take six of us to rescue the damsel, the six of us have to get along. For now.

SON OF THE GODS
I agree with she whose eyes sparkle like Time's first sunset.

(The ASS-KICKING TEEN blushes.)

SON OF THE GODS
No matter our motivations, if we are to rescue this maiden, then we <u>must</u> band together.

SILENT PROTAGONIST
(raising his sword aloft) Iyah!

SON OF THE GODS
For glory!

                    ASS-KICKING TEEN
For justice!

                    BROODING HACKER
For power!

                    BRAVE VOLUNTEER
For family!

                    RELUCTANT BLOND
Wow, I've never seen people so worked up to play a game
before.

                    (The BROODING HACKER, The ASS-KICKING
                    TEEN, The BRAVE VOLUNTEER, and The SON
                    OF THE GODS deflate. The SILENT
                    PROTAGONIST and The RELUCTANT BLOND
                    stay as they are.)

                    BROODING HACKER
To what now?

                    RELUCTANT BLOND
To play a game? Bards & Battlements. *(pulling out another*
scroll) That's what th–...that's what we need six players for.

                    BROODING HACKER
Bards & Battlements? Is that like Dungeons & Dragons?

                    RELUCTANT BLOND
Well, we can't afford to carry official D&D products in the
shop, so this is a...totally different dice-based roleplaying
game.

                    ASS-KICKING TEEN
Oh, one of those nerd games for nerds? I'm not playing that.

BROODING HACKER
Sorry, I'm still trying to wrap my head around this. You got us all together to play a <u>game</u>?

RELUCTANT BLOND
Well, yeah, the…my boss wants us to start hosting some events, so I was looking for other players to run a campaign with me.

BRAVE VOLUNTEER
There are no real, endangered damsels?

RELUCTANT BLOND
Not to my knowledge.

SON OF THE GODS
(grabbing The RELUCTANT BLOND by the lapels) Then **<u>why</u>** did you summon us in such a dramatic manner?

RELUCTANT BLOND
I dunno, I thought it would be immersive!

BROODING HACKER
(reading from the scroll) 'Calling all heroes, adventurers, and otherwise protagonists. The stars have foretold your arrival. Will you answer the call? Come rescue the Damsel of Lucerna Lake and claim your place in history. The fate of the story rests in your ready hands.' *(realizing he didn't read this part before; that makes more sense)* 'Bring your own snacks or something to share.'

ASS-KICKING TEEN
(grabbing The RELUCTANT BLOND's lapels alongside The SON OF THE GODS) But what about the reward?

RELUCTANT BLOND

Ten thousand gold pieces? That's in-game loot – our
characters' reward for completing the quest. Did you think
someone was actually offering gold pieces as currency? For
what, some kind of rescue mission? That's not something
that happens!

ASS-KICKING TEEN

Listen, pal, in the last three weeks, I've closed a fiery portal
in my school's cafeteria, revealed to the school board that
my history teacher's a mummy, and gotten extra evicted
from my apartment, so don't tell me what kinds of things do
and don't happen.

*(The BROODING HACKER grabs a comic book
and holds it hostage.)*

BROODING HACKER

Tell us the truth, blondie, or the merchandise gets it!

RELUCTANT BLOND

No! That's an original Shoebill Man Alpha Print Issue
Number One.

SON OF THE GODS

It's about to be confetti if you don't start making this make
sense.

RELUCTANT BLOND

No, please!

BRAVE VOLUNTEER

Crease the front cover!

*(As The RELUCTANT BLOND reaches full
panic, the room starts to shake, a deep rumbling
bass accompanying his words.)*

RELUCTANT BLOND

No, no, don't! I don't know what more to tell you! I'm just a nerd who works at a comic book store! I thought getting a group together for a team-based roleplaying game would help me make some friends, but apparently I messed it up just like I mess up everything in my life, and I'm sorry! I just wanted to do like it says in the Bards & Battlements handbook and make my life a story worth reading in a world worth saving.

> *(A pause while this all sinks in, the shaking and rumbling fading away. The other Chosen Ones are aware of the rumbling and its departure. The ASS-KICKING TEEN and The SON OF THE GODS release The RELUCTANT BLOND.)*

SON OF THE GODS

How could I have been so brainless? I thought this was a test. One step closer to joining my family on Mount Olympus. But I'm no god. I'm no more than an ordinary fool.

ASS-KICKING TEEN

(playfully teasing) Hey, c'mon. I'm sure you're an extraordinary fool. *(brushing off The RELUCTANT BLOND's lapel)* Sorry about that.

BROODING HACKER

(to The RELUCTANT BLOND) I guess we've got more in common than we thought. My life's not much to read about either.

SILENT PROTAGONIST

(confused at the change in the room's energy) Eeyah?

BRAVE VOLUNTEER

To be fair, I'm not sure how I thought rescuing a damsel was going to keep my family out of danger but…it was exciting to be excited about something for once.

SON OF THE GODS

I suppose I'll have to test my mettle elsewhere.

ASS-KICKING TEEN

Oh, shoot, I've got an AP Chem test tomorrow.

> *(The BROODING HACKER tosses the comic book aside.)*

BROODING HACKER

(to The RELUCTANT BLOND) Next time you wanna make friends, kid, stick to the internet.

BRAVE VOLUNTEER

(seeing how despondent everyone is) Wait wait wait. We can't just abandon this poor, forlorn child.

RELUCTANT BLOND

I'm // nineteen….

BRAVE VOLUNTEER

(taking The RELUCTANT BLOND by the shoulders and talking over him) There may not be a damsel, but surely someone…or something…needs rescuing.

RELUCTANT BLOND

Just my social life, it seems.

BRAVE VOLUNTEER

Well, when you put it that way…perhaps we <u>should</u> play.

RELUCTANT BLOND

Listen, you don't have to–

BRAVE VOLUNTEER

(suddenly completely activated) I will! I'll do it! I volunteer to be the Dungeon Keeper!

RELUCTANT BLOND

A-actually, I was gonna–

BROODING HACKER

You know what? Why not? If she's in, I'm in. It's the least we can do after threatening Shoebill Man number one.

SON OF THE GODS

The stars themselves will tremble at our tabletop might!

ASS-KICKING TEEN

Aw, what the heck. If I can make friends with the chess club, I can get into a little roleplay.

SILENT PROTAGONIST

Hiiyuh!

BROODING HACKER

What'd'ya say, kid? You wanna play some Bards & Battlements or what?

RELUCTANT BLOND

(reluctantly) Well… *(with a swell of bravery)* Alright. Let's give it a one-shot!

> *(The BROODING HACKER, The ASS-KICKING TEEN, The BRAVE VOLUNTEER, and The SON OF THE GODS cheer, patting The RELUCTANT BLOND on the back, ruffling his hair or*

something. The SILENT PROTAGONIST strikes
a pose with his fists on his hips.)

RELUCTANT BLOND
I'll get the sourcebook.

(The RELUCTANT BLOND goes behind the
counter and produces the sourcebook for
Damsel of Lucerna Lake. The other Chosen
Ones make themselves at home.)

RELUCTANT BLOND
And, uh...maybe I could take the lead on this first session? It
was my idea after all.

ASS-KICKING TEEN
(teasing) Ooh, lookit mister 'I have a job' over here.

BRAVE VOLUNTEER
I accept your demotion to player with humility and grace.

RELUCTANT BLOND
I wouldn't say it's a demotion–

SON OF THE GODS
Open the book, cartoon merchant. What wait'st thou for?

RELUCTANT BLOND
Sorry, I'm just nervous. I've never done this with strangers
before.

(The other Chosen Ones huddle around The
RELUCTANT BLOND.)

ASS-KICKING TEEN
Cool book.

BRAVE VOLUNTEER
Looks perilous.

BROODING HACKER
Looks expensive.

ASS-KICKING TEEN
(on closer observation) Looks…ancient. *(to The
RELUCTANT BLOND)* Where'd you say this came from?

RELUCTANT BLOND
(realizing) I don't know, actually. It just kind of appeared on
the counter one day and I've been really compelled to open it
ever since.

BRAVE VOLUNTEER
But you haven't?

RELUCTANT BLOND
Well, no, I mean what's the point without a full adventuring
party?

ASS-KICKING TEEN
An ancient, mysterious book suddenly shows up in your
store accompanied by an inexplicable desire to interact with
it? I've got a bad feeling about this.

SON OF THE GODS
Oh, come now, she whose hair teaches the sun to shine
brightly. What could possibly go wrong?

> *(The SON OF THE GODS yanks The
> RELUCTANT BLOND's hands so that the book
> opens. As soon as he does, The RELUCTANT
> BLOND cannot let go of the book and the shop
> is filled with noise and flashing lights. The room
> shakes as comic books fall from their shelves.*

*The Chosen Ones all keep their footing, but the
CUSTOMER in the background falls over.
Finally, everything stops and the scene is silent
and still.)*

CUSTOMER
(after a moment) **What the heck was that**??

*(The bell rings from the door SL as The
OVERTHINKER enters menacingly. He strides
forward, his focus is on The Chosen Ones, and
he waves a hand dismissively at The
CUSTOMER.)*

OVERTHINKER
You may go.

CUSTOMER
…do I have to or…?

OVERTHINKER
(not what he was expecting) What?

CUSTOMER.
stammering) Y-you said I <u>could</u> go but I don't wanna go I'm
not done pickin' out my comics yet.

*(The OVERTHINKER ponders for a moment,
then waves a hand again.)*

OVERTHINKER
You may stay.

CUSTOMER
Thank you!

(The OVERTHINKER approaches the counter where The Chosen Ones have subconsciously arranged themselves into a protective little huddle.)

OVERTHINKER
I'm here for them anyway.

(The Chosen Ones stand strong and each try to get in the first line of combative dialogue. None of their lines particularly stand out over the others. Sonically, it's just a mess.)

BROODING HACKER
(simultaneous) You walked into the wrong comic shop, pal–
ASS-KICKING TEEN. *(simultaneous)* Get a load of Mister Tall, Dark, and Not So Handsome–
SILENT PROTAGONIST. *(simultaneous)* Hrrrrrrrrrrrrrrrr–
RELUCTANT BLOND. *(simultaneous)* Listen, mister, we don't want any trouble–
BRAVE VOLUNTEER. *(simultaneous)* If you try to harm any innocents on my watch–
SON OF THE GODS. *(simultaneous)* Prepare to be stricken by the power of–

(The Chosen Ones realize they're talking over each other, look at each other, look back at The OVERTHINKER, then huddle up forming a semi-circle that excludes The OVERTHINKER but includes the audience.)

SON OF THE GODS
What are you doing?

BROODING HACKER
I was trying to get in a cheeky one-liner.

ASS-KICKING TEEN
Well, get in <u>line</u>, so was <u>I</u>.

RELUCTANT BLOND
You guys can go first. I was just gonna ask him to leave.

ASS-KICKING TEEN
Well, <u>one</u> of us has to jab him with a quick quip, or else what's the point?

BRAVE VOLUNTEER
Perhaps there is an equitable way to settle this.

SILENT PROTAGONIST
(raising a fist in offering) Hyah?

> *(The other Chosen Ones consider and then agree. They silently play a six-person game of Rock, Paper, Scissors, going on 'Rock, Paper, Scissor, Shoot'. The SON OF THE GODS shoots Rock, The BROODING HACKER shoots Scissors, The ASS-KICKING TEEN shoots Scissors, The RELUCTANT BLOND shoots Paper, The BRAVE VOLUNTEER shoots Paper, and The SILENT PROTAGONIST shoots Rock.)*

BROODING HACKER*(simultaneous)* These are actually laser scissors that cut through rock and light paper on fire, so–
ASS-KICKING TEEN. *(simultaneous)* I once defeated a bigfoot with nothing but a pair of scissors, so I think–
SILENT PROTAGONIST. *(simultaneous)* Hyyyyyyyyah! Ha hup! Hyya!
RELUCTANT BLOND. *(simultaneous)* I knew this wasn't going to work with this many people, but maybe if we do–

BRAVE VOLUNTEER. *(simultaneous)* There is nothing more dangerous to systems of oppression than the power of paper, so–
SON OF THE GODS. *(simultaneous)* I created a rock so heavy that even I couldn't lift it, so obviously it should–

OVERTHINKER

Silence!!

> *(The Chosen Ones turn to face The OVERTHINKER, shocked into silence, except:)*

RELUCTANT BLOND
(from out of the dim; not having realized quickly enough) –
best two out of three… oh.

OVERTHINKER

I will tell you who I am. **I** am your doom. **I** am your demise.
I am The Overthinker!

> *(None of The Chosen Ones know quite how to react to this, so they don't. Or they do with a little confusion and titled heads.)*

OVERTHINKER
(caught off-guard that they're not reacting) What?

> *(The Chosen Ones look among themselves. Somehow The RELUCTANT BLOND gets volunteered as the next one to speak. He works here, after all.)*

RELUCTANT BLOND

Well, it's just…you say that like we're supposed to have heard of you. And I don't think any of us have. Are you…a band or something?

(That wasn't what he was supposed to say. The other Chosen Ones react with frustration.)

BROODING HACKER. *(simultaneous)* **How could a guy be a band**??
ASS-KICKING TEEN. *(simultaneous; sarcastically)* Very intimidating, big guy.
SILENT PROTAGONIST. *(simultaneous)* Hyyah! Huh! Hup!
RELUCTANT BLOND. *(simultaneous)* I'm sorry, I didn't know what to say–!
BRAVE VOLUNTEER. *(simultaneous)* That wasn't menacing at all!
SON OF THE GODS. *(simultaneous; praying)* If anyone's there, save me from these fools–

OVERTHINKER

Silence!!!

(The Chosen Ones are all successfully stunned into silence this time. The OVERTHINKER paces around them as he monologues.)

OVERTHINKER
(facetiously) Am I to understand that one of these <u>bickering fools</u> could alter the balance of the universe? How incredibly unlikely.

ASS-KICKING TEEN
(to the other Chosen Ones) I don't like the look of this guy.

BROODING HACKER
Don't get too close; I bet you wouldn't like the smell of him either.

OVERTHINKER

But here you are. In the flesh. And seeing you face-to-face like this, I wonder why I ever concerned myself with the likes of you. Small. Insignificant. And soon to be destroyed. I will wipe your names from the book of time as easily as I will wipe your bodies from the face of this planet.

SON OF THE GODS

You'll have to kill us first!

BRAVE VOLUNTEER

I <u>think</u> that's what he's implying.

OVERTHINKER

And here I thought there might be some risk in gathering you all. But no, it turns out the sum of your parts is even more incompetent than you were on your own.

ASS-KICKING TEEN

<u>You</u> gathered us?

SON OF THE GODS

And who are you calling uncompotent?

BROODING HACKER

Yeah, check your facts, pal. Blondie over here got us together.

OVERTHINKER

(severely) That's just what I wanted you to **think**. But The Overthinker can put a thought inside your head as easily as you can turn a tap. I planted the module within this very shop. I directed the wind to blow those scrolls into each of your paths. *(to The RELUCTANT BLOND)* Did you think you would ever be brave enough to commune with strangers in such a dramatic fashion without an outside influence? I crept inside your mind and inspired you to reach out, gave

OVERTHINKER (CONT)

you every word to entice foolish heroes into action. Your only contribution was… *(mocking)* 'Bring snacks or something else to share.'

RELUCTANT BLOND

(realizing; of The Chosen Ones) …and none of you did.

OVERTHINKER

But now that you are gathered, I will destroy you all and have no more reason to fear The Prophecy.

(The Chosen One's collective ears perk up at this.)

SON OF THE GODS

Prophecy?

RELUCTANT BLOND

What prophecy?

OVERTHINKER

The Prophecy, you know-nothings!

BROODING HACKER

Like, capital T, capital P, "The Prophecy?"

OVERTHINKER

Yes! An ancient story carved into the bones of the universe that tells of rising strength…and calamitous downfall. The blueprints of how I will destroy your world and become the most powerful being in the universe!

ASS-KICKING TEEN

Hey, this is the first we're hearing of it. That's not fair!

OVERTHINKER

Fair?? FAIR?? The universe isn't fair. How would it be fair
that I should have my greatness threatened by one of you...
mortals?

BROODING HACKER

One of us is supposed to bring you down?

SILENT PROTAGONIST

Hyah?

SON OF THE GODS

And, hey, I'm only half-mortal, so let's watch it with the
name calling.

ASS-KICKING TEEN

But wait, which one of us is destined to kick your butt?

BRAVE VOLUNTEER

I volunteer as butt-kicker!

OVERTHINKER

(incredulously) You don't know? You don't even know
which of you is The Chosen One?

> *(The OVERTHINKER is overcome with
> laughter.)*

OVERTHINKER

Never heard of The Prophecy, don't even know which one of
you is destined for greatness. Some savior you'll turn out to
be, *(giddily; pointing at a different Chosen One with each)* or
you, or you, or you or you or you.

> *(The OVERTHINKER erupts in another gale of
> laughter.)*

ASS-KICKING TEEN
Well, maybe we're all The Chosen One. Did you ever think of that?

OVERTHINKER
(suddenly very serious; maybe a little too hot) Of course I thought of it. I think of more in an instant than you will in your pathetic little lifetime. *(recovering)* But no. There can only be one of you. Or perhaps…a new thought. Perhaps I was wrong. Perhaps it's none of you at all. Perhaps there is…another.

> *(The OVERTHINKER casually picks up the original Shoebill Man alpha print number one.)*

OVERTHINKER
Think think think. Well, wouldn't that be something? The real Chosen One out there somewhere, making you all meaningless simply by existing. And by destroying the six of you and assuring myself of victory, I would be setting the stage for my own ironic failure. *(calculating)* No. You may live…for now. Until I can decide who the true chosen one is. And in the meantime…if any of you try to stand in my way…

> *(The OVERTHINKER tears the comic book in half slowly as he makes his final threat)*

OVERTHINKER
I will tear your reality to pieces.

> *(The OVERTHINKER lets the halves of the comic book fall as The RELUCTANT BLOND shrieks.)*

RELUCTANT BLOND
Original Shoebill Man alpha print issue one, nooo!

(The OVERTHINKER swoops toward the SL doorway.)

OVERTHINKER

Stay out of my way "Chosen Ones," or you'll wish for so swift a demise.

(The OVERTHINKER exits with a whirl of his cape and another menacing laugh, the bell of the door ringing in his wake. There is a light rumble, perhaps the echo of laughter, before all is silent and still in the comic book shop once more. The CUSTOMER walks over to the counter.)

CUSTOMER

Wow, I'm really glad I stayed for that after all. What a show. *(digs in his pocket for money and pays for his comic books)* Sorry about your original Shoebill Man alpha print number one, that stinks. You guys have fun figuring out which one of you is The Chosen One and how to save the world. *(walking toward the door)* Man, I do not envy any of you.

(The CUSTOMER exits with another ring of the bell.)

BROODING HACKER

(slowly coming to terms with what just happened) One of us…is The Chosen One.

BRAVE VOLUNTEER

Not just a hero.

ASS-KICKING TEEN

Not just a savior.

BROODING HACKER
The capital C, capital O, Chosen One.

RELUCTANT BLOND
I'm not sure about this....

SON OF THE GODS
(meaning himself) I mean, come on, I think we've got a
pretty good idea which one of us it is.

BROODING HACKER
We really don't. If __that__ guy didn't know, it could be any of
us.

SILENT PROTAGONIST
Hyah, hup?

> *(The RELUCTANT BLOND has a proper freak
> out and splits from the group.)*

RELUCTANT BLOND
This is crazy!!

ASS-KICKING TEEN
Slow down, tiger. We're all in this together.

RELUCTANT BLOND
Not me! I'm not in anything with anyone! **You** guys can play
savior all you want, but **my** life was perfectly normal until
you all showed up. Comin' in here grabbin' people, sayin'
snarky quips, rippin' comic books in half. That's not me!
That's not what I do! I'm not a hero. I work retail!

> *(The BROODING HACKER, The ASS-KICKING
> TEEN, and The BRAVE VOLUNTEER share a
> look. They've all worked retail; they get it. The*

SILENT PROTAGONIST *is blissfully unaware.*
The SON OF THE GODS *is smarmily unaware.)*

SON OF THE GODS
So we leave him behind. You heard what The Over**stinker**
said: at the end of the day, only one of us matters.

BRAVE VOLUNTEER
I think he's wrong. We all have a part to play in this.

BROODING HACKER
You'll be safer with us, kid, I can promise you that. If he
finds you out there on your own, he might just pick you off
for fun.

RELUCTANT BLOND
But, but–

(The ASS-KICKING TEEN *puts a hand on The*
RELUCTANT BLOND's *shoulder.)*

ASS-KICKING TEEN
Hey. You can trust us. Life's thrown me its fair share of
curveballs too. I've broken curses, thwarted alien invasions –
I even tried out for the cheerleading team with a twisted
ankle, and you know what happened?

RELUCTANT BLOND
How would I know // what–?

ASS-KICKING TEEN.
(interrupting) I made the team. Because my friends
distracted the judges and made it look like I did the best. I
guess what I'm trying to say is: it takes a lot of girls to make
a human pyramid, but there's only room for one at the top.
Will you at least stick around and be a body we can climb
on?

RELUCTANT BLOND

I uh…

ASS-KICKING TEEN

It's like you said: Let's make your life a story worth reading in a world worth saving.

> *(This fills The RELUCTANT BLOND with the resolve he needs.)*

RELUCTANT BLOND

Okay. I'll do it.

BRAVE VOLUNTEER

That's the spirit!

SON OF THE GODS

Fine. More human shields for me.

BROODING HACKER
(to The ASS-KICKING TEEN) Hell of a pep talk.

SILENT PROTAGONIST

Hyeh! Ha?

BROODING HACKER

I hate that I'm starting to understand this guy, but I think he's right. First thing we've gotta do is learn more about this Prophecy nonsense if any of us are going to stand a chance at saving the world. Anyone got the phone number of a good prophecies expert?

ASS-KICKING TEEN

I'd suggest my school's library, but it's infested with pixies.

BRAVE VOLUNTEER
We must rescue the books from these pixie fiends!

BROODING HACKER
No, don't get distracted. We gotta find someone fast.
Someone with a lot of ancient knowledge. A connection to
the primal forces of the universe. Someone it would make
arguably more sense to send on this kind of mission than any
of us.

SON OF THE GODS
(smugly) I think I know just the guy....

> *(The SON OF THE GODS stands smiling and
> nodding at the thought of it. A pause while the
> other Chosen Ones look around between
> themselves and him in confusion.)*

ASS-KICKING TEEN
Okay, who?

SON OF THE GODS
(snapping out of it) Oh, sorry, sorry, follow me.

> *(The Chosen Ones all exit the comic book shop
> SL, the bell ringing as they do. The
> RELUCTANT BLOND is the last to leave, and as
> he does, he turns and takes one last longing look
> at the shop. He inhales and exits. One last bell
> ring. Blackout.)*

ACT I, SCENE IV
A temple to Zeus.

*The comic book shop gets swept away and
replaced with big marble columns. The lights
are dim, like candlelight, and a reverent hum or
soft chanting can be heard.*

The Chosen Ones enter SL.

SON OF THE GODS
(calling out) Dad! I'm home.

BROODING HACKER
Why is there an ancient Greek Parthenon on the outskirts of
the city?

ASS-KICKING TEEN
What do I look like, part of the zoning committee?

SON OF THE GODS
It's not a Parthenon – that's for one of my moms, Athena.
<u>This</u> is a good old-fashioned temple to the main man, the
shape-shifting centerpiece, the thane of the thunderbolt, my
dad – well, one of them anyway – *(takes center facing
upstage and strikes a pose to summon:)* Zeus!

*(There is a tremendous crash of noise, color, and
light from upstage in the rafters. The Chosen
Ones, except The SON OF THE GODS, recoil in
pain and fear at its magnificence.)*

GOD FATHER
(offstage; with a roll of thunder) Is that my son??

SON OF THE GODS
The one and only.

GOD FATHER
(offstage) Well, I wouldn't go that far.

SON OF THE GODS
Okay, well then, your favorite.

GOD FATHER.
offstage) Iiiii–...

SON OF THE GODS
Alright, well, we've got company, so. *(looking around at his agonized companions)* Make yourself decent so mortal eyes may comprehend thee, or whatever.

> *(The upstage display fades as The GOD FATHER enters SR with neither pomp nor circumstance. The other Chosen Ones start to recover with varying levels of speed. The GOD FATHER approaches The SON OF THE GODS and wraps him up in a big bear hug.)*

GOD FATHER
It's been a long time, my boy. Why it seems like only yesterday you were praying to Hermes for help finding your lost retainer.

SON OF THE GODS
Dad, not in front of my companions.

GOD FATHER
(releasing The SON OF THE GODS and turning to the other Chosen Ones) Hello there. You all friends of my boy?

BROODING HACKER. *(simultaneous)* I'm a bit of a loner.

ASS-KICKING TEEN. *(simultaneous)* 'Friends' is, yeah, probably as far as I'd go.
SILENT PROTAGONIST. *(simultaneous; bows)* Hup.
RELUCTANT BLOND*(simultaneous)* I mean, I wouldn't want to presume, but...
BRAVE VOLUNTEER. *(simultaneous)* If a friend is what he requires, then yes.
SON OF THE GODS. *(simultaneous)* You always do this when I bring people over.

GOD FATHER
And what brings you to my humble abode?

RELUCTANT BLOND
We need your hel–...

SON OF THE GODS
(interrupting) Bup bup bup. Play it cool. *(to The GOD FATHER)* We need your help.

GOD FATHER
Go on.

ASS-KICKING TEEN
The world may be in dang–...

SON OF THE GODS
(interrupting again) Up bup bup bup! Play it cool! *(to The GOD FATHER)* The world may be in danger.

GOD FATHER
Go on.

BROODING HACKER
What do you know about The Proph–

SON OF THE GODS
(interrupting once more) Up bup bup bup bup! <u>Play</u> <u>it</u> <u>cool</u>.
(to The GOD FATHER) What do you know about…The
Prophecy?

GOD FATHER
(with sudden rage) The Prophecy?!?

> *(The GOD FATHER swings his arm and
> summons a bolt of lightning that crashes down
> on The SON OF THE GODS. It is a massive and
> impressive light and sound display, and The
> SON OF THE GODS reacts with an almost-
> cartoonish full-body spasm.)*

GOD FATHER
How dare you speak of such notorious portents within these
hallowed halls??

SON OF THE GODS
(coughing up a puff of smoke) Next time, one of you guys
take the lead.

BRAVE VOLUNTEER
Apologies, O mighty all-father.

GOD FATHER
Please, my father's father was the all-father. Just call me Big
Z.

BRAVE VOLUNTEER
I don't…think so, no. But is there somewhere…less
hallowed that we could talk about this? We really need to
know about the, uh…*(not wanting to get struck by lightning)*
capital T capital P.

GOD FATHER

Well…why not? Any disciples of my son's are disciples of mine.

BROODING HACKER

We're not–

SON OF THE GODS

(interrupting) Thanks, dad.

GOD FATHER

But not here. We'll have to speak somewhere more secure…

> *(The GOD FATHER snaps his fingers. The architecture of the temple disappears, either by unseen forces or the scurrying efforts of the backstage crew. In either case, The Chosen Ones look around at the transformation in amazement.)*

ASS-KICKING TEEN

(in wonder; maybe it echoes) Where are we?

GOD FATHER

A liminal space. Where no plot devices can harm us or interfere with this monumental info dump. I call it…The Cave of Transformation and Good Vibes Only.

BROODING HACKER

Spacious.

GOD FATHER

Yes, I've spent a lot of time here in the last decade and a half. Thinking. Praying. Sorting through exposition.

SON OF THE GODS

Both of my moms said you were away on a work trip–

GOD FATHER

That's not important now. What is important is...The
Prophecy.

(The GOD FATHER reveals a scroll that rolls
out to an impossible length. The Chosen Ones
watch it as it continues to unfurl even offstage
left.)

RELUCTANT BLOND

(whining) This is gonna take forever.

GOD FATHER

(with a chuckle) Worry not, mortal. We gods are old and our
eyesight is going, so it's just a really big font.

(The GOD FATHER reveals that, yes, The
Prophecy is printed on this scroll in a huge font,
something like one letter per line.)

GOD FATHER

Now, I must warn you. Ancient unknowable knowledge can
often be more of a curse than a boon. You're sure you're
ready to hear this?

BROODING HACKER

(smarmily; taking focus) I always am.

GOD FATHER

Okay... That's him, what about the rest of you?

ASS-KICKING TEEN. (casually, almost mumbling;
simultaneously) Yeah, I mean, 'ready' is definitely
subjective, but sure.

RELUCTANT BLOND. *(casually, almost mumbling; simultaneously)* I guess if we have to; I still don't even know what I'm doin' here.
SILENT PROTAGONIST. *(casually, almost mumbling; simultaneously)* Hyup ha! Hayup! Hrr.
BRAVE VOLUNTEER. *(casually, almost mumbling; simultaneously)* I fear no scroll nor ink. I am ready to receive this knowledge.
SON OF THE GODS. *(casually, almost mumbling; simultaneously)* Lay it on us, daddio, sorry I don't know why I said that like that.

GOD FATHER
(cocking an eyebrow) Good enough. *(clears his throat; reading)* "Before there was Time, there was…**The Prophecy**. And so it was written…"

> *(The Powers That Be enter. What follows as The Prophecy is spoken is the best audio/visual display your production can produce. Lights, sounds, projections – a flowing miasma that depicts the words, events, and emotions of The Prophecy in a way that underscores, underlines, and highlights its magnitude without drawing away from the words themselves. Or nothing and you can ignore this stage direction. Honestly, if the words can't portray what they're supposed to convey, what am I even doing here?)*

PTB ALL
…and so it shall be!

PTB 1
For as long as there have been forces of creation, there have also been forces of destruction. One day there will arise a power not only capable of destruction, but able to end the very act of creation itself.

PTB 2
And against that power, a hero shall rise! The power will be known by its desire for silence. And the hero will be known by the company they keep.

PTB 3
And should that hero fail, the power will rule, and everything shall end.

RELUCTANT BLOND
Everything??

PTB ALL
(with finality) **Everything**.

PTB 1
And when the power shall first show its face, the true hero will falter.

PTB 2
But by their rising up, events shall be put into motion unseen and unknown.

PTB 3
A mountain must be climbed, both of earth and of the mind.

PTB 1
For a party shall be formed of strangers who become friends.

PTB 2
And they shall seek out a series of old men who shall aid in their efforts, each with a beard that is longer and whiter than the last.

PTB 3

And at the eleventh second of the eleventh minute of the eleventh hour of the eleventh day of the eleventh week of the eleventh month of the eleventh year of the eleventh era, The Chosen One shall emerge. And the day shall be well and truly saved.

PTB 1

So it was…

PTB 2

…is…

PTB 3

…and forever will be."

PTB

(breaking character a bit; to PTB 3) And, just to say it out loud, you're getting <u>much</u> better at this.

PTB 3

(genuinely but still presenting) **<u>Thank</u>** you.

PTB 2

This has been…

PTB ALL

The Prophecy!

> *(The display fades away as The Powers That Be exit, waving their arms mysteriously and making unknowable little noises. The GOD FATHER rolls or tosses the scroll offstage as The Chosen Ones recover.)*

GOD FATHER

So. That's that.

SILENT PROTAGONIST
Huuuuuu....

BROODING HACKER
What he said.

ASS-KICKING TEEN
Yeah, that didn't exactly...make things any clearer.

BRAVE VOLUNTEER
But it did point us in a direction of sorts.

GOD FATHER
And, son, you're this "Chosen One?"

SON OF THE GODS
I—

ASS-KICKING TEEN.
(interrupting) We don't know, actually. Which one of us it is.

GOD FATHER
Ah. Well. Good luck with that.

BRAVE VOLUNTEER
It sounds like we have a mountain to climb.

RELUCTANT BLOND
Literally and metaphorically.

GOD FATHER
If an old man with a long white beard might offer some sage advice–...agh!!

(The GOD FATHER clutches his chest and falls to a dramatic position on one knee. The SON OF THE GODS rushes to his side.)

SON OF THE GODS
Father!

(The voice of POSEIDON crashes into the room like a wave.)

POSEIDON
(offstage) Yes?

SON OF THE GODS
What? No, not you, *(indicating The GOD FATHER)* this father.

POSEIDON
(offstage) Oh, my bad.

(With a splash, the voice is gone.)

SON OF THE GODS
(to The GOD FATHER) Are you alright?

GOD FATHER
(struggling to breathe) Far from it, I'm afraid. It seems this force of destruction you face has its claws deeper into the fabric of reality than we could have guessed. Something unseen eats away at my strength, or else I would face this challenge head on. *(takes The SON OF THE GODS' face in his hands)* Son…if it is you who is to be the capital C, capital O Chosen One, you must succeed. And if not, you must ensure that whichever of your companions rises, you will support their journey.

SON OF THE GODS

But dad–

GOD FATHER

'But' me not! And promise.

> *(The SON OF THE GODS looks back at his
> companions, then at The GOD FATHER.)*

SON OF THE GODS

(solemnly) I promise.

GOD FATHER

(to the group) When in doubt, always return to the words of
The Prophecy. The journey ahead of you is long and
dangerous, but stand together and you will stand strong.
Now go!

> *(A huge clap of thunder chases The Chosen
> Ones offstage left. The SON OF THE GODS
> lingers for one moment longer, looking back at
> The GOD FATHER. The GOD FATHER nods
> and The SON OF THE GODS exits. The GOD
> FATHER lingers for a moment, thunder still
> echoing as The OVERTHINKER enters stage
> right.)*

GOD FATHER

How did you get in here?

OVERTHINKER

And here I thought you'd be happy to see me.

GOD FATHER

(struggle to rise) The Cave of Transformation and Good
Vibes Only is no place for interlopers.

OVERTHINKER.
(tutting) Is the god of thunder feeling a bit under the weather?

GOD FATHER
(rising defiantly) Thor is the god of thunder; I'm the god of kicking ass and taking names. *(squaring up)* What's yours?

OVERTHINKER
Oh, me? First name, The. Last name, Last Thing You See Before You Die.

GOD FATHER
(gravely) Wait a minute… *(then, deeply casual)* I recognize that name from high school. Is your father Jeremy Last Thing You See Before You Die?

OVERTHINKER
…no.

> *(The OVERTHINKER rears back and strikes forward at The GOD FATHER. There is a terrible violent sound, a cry of pain from The GOD FATHER, and a BLACKOUT!)*

ACT I, SCENE V
A bus stop.

The park bench from before can get repurposed here as a bench at the bus stop. Maybe there's a sign, maybe a garbage can. The set pieces in this scene are really just to break up the architecture and give the characters some levels to find so they're not all standing around talking. Also so that the audience doesn't think we're in a liminal space, cause we're not, we're at a bus stop.

The Chosen Ones enter SL, fresh from their scatter, and spread out on the stage catching their breaths.

BROODING HACKER
(at The SON OF THE GODS) Remind me not to join you for any family reunions.

SON OF THE GODS
You wouldn't be invited anyway, peasant!

BROODING HACKER
Why I oughta–

ASS-KICKING TEEN
(breaking them up) Knock it off! We've got a world to save.

BROODING HACKER
One of us does.

SON OF THE GODS
Yes, one of us **does**.

BROODING HACKER
(to The SON OF THE GODS) You really think it's you, don't you?

SON OF THE GODS
Why wouldn't it be? I'm the <u>son</u> <u>of</u> <u>the</u> <u>gods</u>! Doesn't get much more pre-ordained than that.

ASS-KICKING TEEN
And how many homecoming dances have <u>you</u> saved lately?

SON OF THE GODS
None, because I don't know what those are!

ASS-KICKING TEEN
Well, maybe **ask** me to one sometime and I'll **show** you!

SON OF THE GODS
(distracted by hormones) Wait, what?

ASS-KICKING TEEN
(distracted by The SON OF THE GODS' distraction) What? Hm?

BROODING HACKER
(to The SILENT PROTAGONIST) Get a load of the 'will-they won't-they' on those two.

SILENT PROTAGONIST
(not quite getting it but happy to be included) Hyah.

BRAVE VOLUNTEER
This squabbling isn't getting us anywhere. Perhaps it's just a decision we should make on our own. I volunteer to be The Chosen One.

BROODING HACKER
I don't think that–

BRAVE VOLUNTEER
(grandly, to the heavens) I VOLUNTEER TO BE THE
CHOSEN ONE!!

> *(The Chosen Ones all look around, checking to
> see if that might have done something.)*

BROODING HACKER
I don't think that's how it works.

RELUCTANT BLOND
How does it work?

BROODING HACKER
Prophetically. Supposedly.

RELUCTANT BLOND
(of The Prophecy) You believe in all that…prophecy
business?

SON OF THE GODS
(correcting him) Not "prophecy business." "Prophecy
business!"

BROODING HACKER
(to The RELUCTANT BLOND) Kid, we just met a god; I'm
not ruling anything out at this point. Now do you want to
avenge your torn-up comic or not?

RELUCTANT BLOND
Fine. Then where do we go from here?

BRAVE VOLUNTEER
Forward.

ASS-KICKING TEEN
Forward where?

BRAVE VOLUNTEER
Toward the mountain.

SON OF THE GODS
Which mountain, pray tell?

BRAVE VOLUNTEER
(frustrated at their lack of momentum) Any mountain!
<u>Choose</u> a mountain! Or let's climb the first mountain we find
and see what's at the top of it! And if that's not the right
mountain, we'll scale another! We will trek the peaks of
every range in the world if that's what it takes to keep our
loved ones safe!

BROODING HACKER
(trying to appease her) While your passion is commendable,
that's not a very appealing plan. Too many variables.

ASS-KICKING TEEN
Wait a minute. *(to The SON OF THE GODS)* Your father
said–

SON OF THE GODS
(gently correcting) <u>One</u> of my fathers.

ASS-KICKING TEEN
(taking the note) One of your fathers said, "When in doubt,
always return to the words of The Prophecy."

BROODING HACKER
Capital T, capital P.

ASS-KICKING TEEN
(quoting) "And they shall seek out a series of old men who shall aid in their efforts…"

RELUCTANT BLOND
(joining in) "…each with a beard that is longer and whiter than the last." Hey, you're right!

SON OF THE GODS
Surely there are none with beards longer or whiter than the chin follicles of the almighty Zeus!

BROODING HACKER
I can think of, like, ten guys off the top of my head that fit that description, Santa Claus included.

SON OF THE GODS
Then we shall find this Santa Claus and demand his assistance.

ASS-KICKING TEEN
(not sure how to break it to him) I'm not…sure he's available this time of year.

BRAVE VOLUNTEER
Help is for those who cannot <u>do</u> for themselves. I will climb this mountain and find this old man on my own.

BROODING HACKER
Hey, if <u>you</u> can do it alone, <u>I</u> can do it alone backwards!

RELUCTANT BLOND
Sorry, have we decided on a mountain?

ASS-KICKING TEEN
This is **<u>exactly</u>** why we need to find a wise old man.

(The BOY WIZARD pops on from SR, wand in hand and ready for adventure.)

BOY WIZARD

I know where you can find a wise old man with a long white beard!

BROODING HACKER. *(simultaneous)* I hope this bus comes early and crushes you, you weird little nobody, get outta here!

ASS-KICKING TEEN. *(simultaneous)* No thank you, and don't think that's polite, it's just my way of saying get lost!

SILENT PROTAGONIST. *(simultaneous)* Hrrrrrrrrr yah! Yah ha hiyah!

RELUCTANT BLOND. *(simultaneous)* Who is this guy? Sorry, there are too many of us already, you should probably go.

BRAVE VOLUNTEER. *(simultaneous)* I swear upon my ancestors, if you don't make like a tree and get the heck outta here–...!

SON OF THE GODS. *(simultaneous)* Leave my sight, magical child, or I shall make thee leave me with my own might!

BOY WIZARD. *(simultaneous, toward the middle of their lines)* I'm sorry, I just thought I could help! You guys are mean!

(The BOY WIZARD exits. The Chosen Ones relax a bit.)

BROODING HACKER

Okay, so. Does anyone else have any idea where to start looking for this wise old man?

(From SL, The FANATIC slinks on and perches on the park bench.)

FANATIC

I know where to look.

*(The Chosen Ones react to this sudden presence,
especially The SILENT PROTAGONIST who
starts rolling and jumping up, leaping into
various offensive and defensive poses.)*

SILENT PROTAGONIST

Hiyup ha! Hyup! Hah! Hyah!

*(The other Chosen Ones calm The SILENT
PROTAGONIST.)*

SON OF THE GODS

(to The SILENT PROTAGONIST) Stay your blade. Let's hear
him out.

RELUCTANT BLOND

(to The FANATIC) Who are you?

FANATIC

Me, sweetness? Ahem. We are– ahem, sorry, ahem, pizza
still caught in throat. Ahem, ahem!

SON OF THE GODS

We shall call you Ahem.

FANATIC

What? No, that's not–...

BROODING HACKER

Cut to the chase, Ahem. What do you know about a bearded
old man who lives on a mountain?

FANATIC

Yesssssss… Big beard. Big white beard. Very wise. Lives at the top of Mount Mood, he does. We can take you to him, sweetness! <u>Ahem</u>! <u>Ahem</u>!

BRAVE VOLUNTEER

What's in it for you?

FANATIC

Nothing, sweetness. We just wants to go on an adventure. Climb up the mountain to see the wise old man – that's adventure, sweetness.

SON OF THE GODS

That's a walk in the park for us.

ASS-KICKING TEEN

Not if we don't know where we're going.

BROODING HACKER

Why don't you just tell us where he is and we'll find our own way there?

FANATIC

Too dangerous, sweetness! Many trials, many enemies. But we know lots of secret shortcuts. We will get you there safely! <u>Ahem</u>!

BRAVE VOLUNTEER

And how do you know such a clear path? Why can't you make us a map?

FANATIC

Can't remember off top of my head, sweetness. Only recognize the way by seeing it, <u>ahem</u>. Have to travel <u>with</u> you.

ASS-KICKING TEEN
I don't know about this….

BROODING HACKER
And I thought blondie was supposed to be the reluctant one.

RELUCTANT BLOND
Hey!

BROODING HACKER
Well, no offense, but I don't exactly see you offering any alternatives.

RELUCTANT BLOND
(to the other Chosen Ones) Don't you see? This has to be some kind of trap. *(of The FANATIC)* Either he has ulterior intentions or following him will hamper our journey and our personal developments. What if we're not ready to face The Overthinker when we find him because we took the first shortcut that presented itself? Shouldn't we tackle our own obstacles? Overcome our own challenges? Rise above our own preconceptions of what we're capable of?

(The other Chosen Ones consider this.)

BROODING HACKER
…nnnno, I think we should go with the guy who knows where he's going.

ASS-KICKING TEEN. *(simultaneous)* Yeah, I'm with the brooding one on this.
SILENT PROTAGONIST. *(simultaneous)* Hup hyah. Hup!
BRAVE VOLUNTEER. *(simultaneous)* There will be time for adversity later, frail one.
SON OF THE GODS. *(simultaneous)* No pain, much gain, my fathers always said.

(The RELUCTANT BLOND inhales.)

RELUCTANT BLOND
Alright. Lead the way, Ahem.

FANATIC
Yes! Yes! We will lead the way, sweetness! Up the mountain and into the maw of adventure. But not over his sharp little teethsies, sweetness. Up, up! Follow, follow! Ahem! Ahem!

(The FANATIC leads The Chosen Ones offstage left. The exiting order is something like The FANATIC, The SILENT PROTAGONIST, The BRAVE VOLUNTEER, The SON OF THE GODS, The BROODING HACKER, with The ASS-KICKING TEEN and The RELUCTANT BLOND lingering in the back of the group.)

ASS-KICKING TEEN
(putting an arm around The RELUCTANT BLOND's shoulder) See? You're starting to get a hang of this adventuring thing.

RELUCTANT BLOND
I guess so.

ASS-KICKING TEEN
This is the way forward. You'll see.

RELUCTANT BLOND
I hope you're right.

(As they exit, a VENDOR enters SR with a tray full of items, like at a baseball game.)

VENDOR

World-saving items here! Get your magical, mystical, world-saving items here! Can't carpe a diem without a deus ex machina! Get 'em while they're guaranteed to alter the course of destiny! No genies' curses, no monkey's paw loopholes, just clean and fresh world-saving items here! First one's free, get 'em while they're here. *(looks around at the empty stage)* Huh. No one? Guess I'll go throw these in a well. Oh well. *(realizing)* Ha. I see what I did there. Well well. Well well well.

> *(The VENDOR continues muttering to himself as he exits SR and the lights fade.)*

ACT I, SCENE VI

At the mouth of a cave atop Mount Mood.

SL is the entrance to The Cave. It is wide and imposing, decorated with stalactites and/or stalagmites as you see fit. The large playing area in front of the mouth of the cave gives the impression of height, as at the top of a mountain.

The Chosen Ones and The FANATIC enter SR.

FANATIC

This is the place, sweetness. See? Easy journey. Easy peasey. <u>Ahem</u>!

BROODING HACKER

Two days of uninterrupted travel. Good job, Ahem. We owe you one.

ASS-KICKING TEEN

And in that time, we've grown closer as people.

SON OF THE GODS

As teammates.

ASS-KICKING TEEN

(to The RELUCTANT BLOND) See? Worth it.

RELUCTANT BLOND

I still think it would have been more satisfying to share that growth with others somehow....

BRAVE VOLUNTEER

(to The FANATIC) So, where is he? Where's the bearded old wise man?

FANATIC
(pointing toward the cave) In there, sweetness. Lives in the cave. Allllll the way at the back.

RELUCTANT BLOND
Now I've got a bad feeling about this.

SON OF THE GODS
Oh, come now, he who trembles like the newborn calf. What could possibly go wrong?

> *(From out of the cave explodes an army of*
> *GRUNTS!, at least six, but ideally one or two*
> *dozen. Creative costuming or cardboard doubles*
> *can help increase the numbers, but our heroes*
> *should feel really overwhelmed by this attack.*
>
> *The Chosen Ones spring into action, defending*
> *themselves against The GRUNTS as much as*
> *possible as The GRUNTS use their superior*
> *numbers to their advantage. The scuffling that's*
> *not in the foreground can be kept to restrained*
> *shuffling or punch-block combos until it's that*
> *Chosen One's time to shine. The FANATIC*
> *watches from the sidelines, their glee becoming*
> *distress as The Chosen Ones gain the upper*
> *hand.*
>
> *First, The ASS-KICKING TEEN handily*
> *dispatches two or more grunts with an*
> *impressive gymnastic display. Then The SON OF*
> *THE GODS uses his god-given powers to*
> *dispatch a few more. They kick ass back-to-back*
> *for a little bit.)*

SON OF THE GODS
Your fighting technique is almost as beautiful as you are.

ASS-KICKING TEEN
Thanks. Ten years of ballet, eight years of tae kwon do, and thirteen summers of horse-riding camp will do that for ya.

> *(They smile at each other. Focus shifts to The BROODING HACKER. He's fending them off as best he can, maybe hacking one of them with a portable computer, but another is about to get him from behind, oh no! Suddenly, The BRAVE VOLUNTEER rescues him by shooting The GRUNT with an arrow! The BROODING HACKER sees that he was saved and then sees who saved him.)*

BROODING HACKER
Thanks, but I can handle myself.

BRAVE VOLUNTEER
Until we know which one of us is The Chosen One, I've got your back whether you like it or not!

> *(They fend off a few more before focus shifts to The SILENT PROTAGONIST and The RELUCTANT BLOND.*
>
> *The RELUCTANT BLOND is mostly cowering and ducking, his attempts to flee leading GRUNTS right into The SILENT PROTAGONIST's attacks. Eventually, while The SILENT PROTAGONIST is engaged, two or more GRUNTs gang up on The RELUCTANT BLOND, who panics. In a moment of sheer desperation, The RELUCTANT BLOND lets loose a powerful scream and flexes his hand at one of the GRUNTs, uses his latent mind powers to lift it off the ground. The GRUNT struggles in*

the air and the rest look on in amazement. The
RELUCTANT BLOND howls as he flings the
GRUNT around for a bit before tossing him
offstage with a mighty crash. The Chosen Ones
are awe-struck, still struggling against the
GRUNTs, but focusing on what just happened.)

BROODING HACKER
What was that??

RELUCTANT BLOND
I don't know…but it felt awesome!!

(The fighting continues, everyone all at once.
The push and pull goes back and forth, but The
GRUNTs are once more getting the upper hand.)

ASS-KICKING TEEN
(calling out in desperation) Ahem! Do something!

FANATIC
Ooh, sorry, sweetness. No can do. The Grunts want to eat
meat, and we provide it for a price.

BROODING HACKER
What?? Ahem, you little traitor!

FANATIC
That's not our name, sweetness! Our name is–!

(A cosmic boom emanates from the mouth of the
cave as The MENTOR emerges, staff in hand.)

MENTOR
(raising his staff) YOU SHALL NOT… *(slamming his staff*
down) DO THAT ANYMORE!

*(The GRUNTs are knocked off their feet! The
Chosen Ones remain upright, but just barely.
The bodies of any manufactured GRUNTs can
remain onstage as the rest retreat. The Chosen
Ones watch in awe as The MENTOR approaches
The FANATIC who recoils in fear.)*

MENTOR
How dare you darken my doorstep, you miserable creature.

FANATIC
Sorry, sir. No harm meant, sweetness. Was just bringing
these heroes to see you, <u>ahem</u>!

MENTOR
And who directed these Grunts to my cave as well, hm?
Thought you'd kill seven birds with a few dozen stones, did
you?

FANATIC
We don't know what you're talking about, sweetness. Must
have misheard us, <u>ahem</u>.

*(The MENTOR raises his staff against The
FANATIC. The FANATIC flinches and The
Chosen Ones react with shock. The MENTOR
lowers his staff and knocks against The
FANATIC's head twice.)*

MENTOR
Two for flinching.

*(Everyone relaxes a bit, but the mood is still
tense and dangerous.)*

MENTOR

If I see you again, I'll turn you into a toad with crippling student loan debt.

(The FANATIC panics and flees. Satisfied, The Mentor turns back to The Chosen Ones.)

MENTOR

Now. I don't remember leaving a welcome mat at my secluded cave entrance. What are you all doing here?

BROODING HACKER. *(simultaneous)* Listen here, gramps, we've come a long way in a short amount of time to—
ASS-KICKING TEEN. *(simultaneous)* We're the answer to your problems and everybody else's so you'd better—
SILENT PROTAGONIST. *(simultaneous)* Hyaaaaaaah ha! Ha! Hyup ha!
RELUCTANT BLOND. *(simultaneous)* Sorry to disturb you, it's just we've really got to figure out this capital C capital O business—
BRAVE VOLUNTEER. *(simultaneous)* We are here to learn at your feet, if you be the one we seek—
SON OF THE GODS. *(simultaneous)* The glory you see before you in none other than the savior of this and many worlds—

(The MENTOR raises a hand, and The Chosen Ones stop speaking. The MENTOR holds up one finger, indicating that only one of them should speak. The Chosen Ones look among themselves and volunteer The ASS-KICKING TEEN to step forward.)

ASS-KICKING TEEN

We're looking for a wise old man with a beard longer and whiter than that of Zeus himself to be our guide. Do you know him?

MENTOR

Of course I know him. You're lookin' at him.

ASS-KICKING TEEN

We need your help. One of us is The Chosen One.

MENTOR

Capital C, capital O?

ASS-KICKING TEEN

Yes. And we need to better understand The Prophecy.

MENTOR

Capital T, capital P?

ASS-KICKING TEEN

Yes, can you help us?

MENTOR

Capital N, capital O.

*(The MENTOR turns and starts walking back
toward the mouth of The Cave.)*

ASS-KICKING TEEN

(taking a moment to understand) Wh–...wait, **no**??

BROODING HACKER

What do you mean, no?

(The MENTOR turns back.)

MENTOR

Guys, I live in a cave. I'm old. I got creepy little guys bringin' all kindsa little googahs around my place. I'm <u>old</u>. I just wanna be left in peace so I don't have to die and come back in a different form.

RELUCTANT BLOND

Is that what happens when you die?

MENTOR

Not <u>you</u>. That's what happens when <u>I</u> die. I'm super old and magical and stuff, so when I die I'll come back in a new form, with a new name, and then I gotta change, like, all my driver's licenses and stuff. It's a big hassle. If one of <u>you</u> dies, you're just dead. And I don't wanna be a part of that either.

ASS-KICKING TEEN

But we've come a long way just to see you!

MENTOR

Did you? Or did you follow that freak up the shortcut side of the mountain? Name one peril you faced along the way. One lesson you learned?

(The Chosen Ones are embarrassed that they can't think of anything.)

MENTOR

Yeah, I didn't think so. The <u>real</u> Chosen One is probably out there right now making allies and thwarting enemies, not skating by on the <u>presumption</u> of greatness. *(turning to go)* Good day.

BROODING HACKER

(turning to go) Come on, guys–

MENTOR
(turning back; fiercely) **I said 'Good day!'**

BROODING HACKER
(turning back) I **know**! That's why we're **leaving**!

MENTOR
Oh. Sorry, most people…usually push back a little more.

BROODING HACKER
No, you win. Enjoy your cave. *(turning to go; to the other Chosen Ones)* Come on, guys. We'll find someone with a longer, whiter beard.

MENTOR
Wait!

> *(The Chosen Ones stop in their tracks and turn back.)*

MENTOR
(gravely) …say that again.

> *(The BROODING HACKER is momentarily taken off-guard by someone using his own quip against him, but quickly recovers with a smirk.)*

BROODING HACKER
Oh yeah, didn't we mention? You're not the only wizened old fart out there.

ASS-KICKING TEEN
(quoting) "And they shall seek out a <u>series</u> of old men who shall aid in their efforts…"

RELUCTANT BLOND
(finishing up) "...each with a beard that is longer and whiter than the last."

BRAVE VOLUNTEER
There could be hundreds of other mentors out there for us to find.

SON OF THE GODS
Dozens even.

BRAVE VOLUNTEER
(aside to The SON OF THE GODS) That's less than what I said.

SON OF THE GODS
(not getting it) Yeah! That's <u>less</u> than what she said!

SILENT PROTAGONIST
Hup, ha!

MENTOR
You really do know The Prophecy, eh?

BROODING HACKER
Every word.

SON OF THE GODS
'Bring snacks or something else to share.'

ASS-KICKING TEEN
(wrong prophecy) No, that's not–. Never mind.

BROODING HACKER
One of us is destined. For greatness. For <u>something</u>. And we're not going to stop until we find the right bearded old man. *(to The MENTOR)* So you can either rot away here in

BROODING HACKER (CONT)

your little cave, alone and ineffective, frightened of your own transformation, or you can get off your magical dumper and be a partner of greatness.

> *(The MENTOR is shaking with fury. After a moment, he turns and storms off into The Cave. The Chosen Ones sigh with regret – they really thought they had him.)*

BROODING HACKER

Well–

> *(The MENTOR explodes back into the room with a blast of sound and light. He is carrying way more than he ought to be able to: weapons, artifacts, schematics, and he dumps them all majestically out in front of him.)*

MENTOR

Who's ready to save the world??

> *(The Chosen Ones all cheer. The MENTOR starts passing out weapons and artifacts to the party as he lectures them.)*

MENTOR

Rule number one: know thy enemy. Who we goin' up against?

SON OF THE GODS

The villain calls himself The Overthinker.

MENTOR

Ooh, hate to hear it – that guy's gonna be one step ahead of us the whole time. Anybody know the weakness of an overthinker?

ASS-KICKING TEEN
Anti-anxiety medication?

MENTOR
Close. Underthinking. Gut instinct. You're gonna do what
you do best and that should be enough to bring you face-to-
face.

RELUCTANT BLOND
But shouldn't we grow and change as a part of our journey? I
just learned I've got some kind of…latent telekinetic ability.

MENTOR
And how did you manifest it?

RELUCTANT BLOND
Well, I don't know, I just…did.

MENTOR
Exactly! I don't want to undercut the work you've got to do,
but at the end of the day, you've got to trust in yourselves
and trust in each other. How long have you all known each
other?

BRAVE VOLUNTEER
Not long at all, but already some of us are starting to feel
like family.

MENTOR
Careful with that. He could use those feelings against you.
Put one of you in danger as leverage against the others.
Force you to make a deal of impossible choices. That's the
kind of work overthinkers do.

BROODING HACKER
So we should stay emotionally distant. *(He likes the sound of that.)*

MENTOR
(correcting him) Can't do that either. If you're not a cohesive unit, he'll pry at your individual weaknesses until he manages to turn you all against each other. Squabbling, in-fighting, other third-act conflicts. What you've got to do is be true to yourselves and stick together. Whichever one of you is the Chosen One will reveal itself in time. Do I make myself clear?

(The SILENT PROTAGONIST gives a solemn nod.)

MENTOR
Good, now take these tools and triumph! Find and defeat each of The Overthinker's three underbosses – that'll lead you straight to his fortress. *(parenthetically)* He's a dangerous adversary, but not a terribly original thinker. *(no longer parenthetically)* By the time you face him, you should have found enough growth and developed enough character to stop this fiend for good. Now, get outta here, and be better than you've ever been before!

RELUCTANT BLOND
Aren't you coming with us?

MENTOR
I can't! *(gesturing to the cave mouth)* If those Grunts come back, they could use the rest of this arsenal to really wreak some havoc. Besides, I'm not The Chosen One. *(proudly)* One of you is. Now… *(waving his arms and shooing them off)* Fly, you geese!

(As The Chosen Ones exit, they give a battle cry. The MENTOR holds The BROODING HACKER back for a moment with his words.)

MENTOR

And thank you…for reminding me what it feels like to do something useful.

BROODING HACKER

Don't mention it, old timer.

(The BROODING HACKER turns to go. The MENTOR stops him again.)

MENTOR

And one more thing…if you do find someone else out there with a longer, whiter beard than mine…don't tell me.

(The BROODING HACKER chuckles and nods.)

BROODING HACKER

You got it.

(The BROODING HACKER turns to go but holds himself back this time.)

BROODING HACKER

Hey, can I ask you something?

MENTOR

Of course.

BROODING HACKER

Why do you live up here in this cave on the top of a mountain all by yourself?

MENTOR

Oh, me? *(after a moment of consideration)* I guess I'm just a bit of a loner.

> *(The BROODING HACKER takes this in, nods, and exits. The MENTOR stands alone for a moment, watching them leave. The OVERTHINKER enters from The Cave.)*

OVERTHINKER

You can't stop me, you know.

MENTOR

Oh, I know. But one of <u>them</u> can. Someone should have a long time ago.

OVERTHINKER

Why don't you do something about it now?

MENTOR

Because you're not real. You're not here right now. You never were. <u>Father</u>.

OVERTHINKER

What?

> *(The MENTOR turns.)*

MENTOR

Oh, sorry, I thought you were someone else.

OVERTHINKER

Why don't you leave the thinking to <u>me</u>?

> *(A blade bursts through The MENTOR as The OVERTHINKER runs him through. The MENTOR is shocked, but accepts his fate as he*

dies. The OVERTHINKER laughs as The MENTOR slumps to the ground and falls. Blackout.)

ACT I. SCENE VII

A liminal space.

The mouth of The Cave is gone. We're in a new liminal space, where the design indicates the passage of space and time: moving lights, warping sounds, etc. – it's a montage.

The Powers That Be enter and take positions around the stage. As they speak, The Chosen Ones enter and move through the space, as a clump, as a line, as a unit, enacting travel and the actions that The Powers That Be describe.

PTB 1

And so it was that The Chosen Ones set out to test themselves against the forces that would stand against them.

PTB 2

They used their inherent strengths, bolstered by The Mentor's wisdom and the skills of their partners, to defeat many enemies.

PTB 1

They struck down the Ravenous Maw, a feral beast in the Overthinker's employ.

(The Chosen Ones fight and defeat The RAVENOUS MAW. It is a thrilling fight.)

PTB 2

They defeated The Overthinker's mightiest warriors, The Toxic Triad Sisters.

(The Chosen Ones fight and defeat The TOXIC TRIAD SISTERS. It is a perilous fight.)

PTB 3

They fought some guy named Jeff that The Overthinker paid twenty bucks to get in their way.

> *(The Chosen Ones fight JEFF. It is ... an embarrassing fight.)*

PTB 1

And with their foe's underbosses defeated, they were brought to the lair of The Overthinker himself.

PTB 2

But even if they could breach his unrelenting fortress, they would not find their foe within.

PTB 1

No, for this destructive antagonist had been busy, vanquishing gods and murdering mentors.

PTB 3

And now he meant to disrupt the very fabric of time by siphoning the energy of The Powers That Be themselves.

PTB 1

(did not see that coming) Wait, what?

> *(The OVERTHINKER enters cackling and launches himself at The Powers The Be. Beams from his fingertips sap the energy from them as they writhe in agony.)*

PTB 1

How are you...doing this?

OVERTHINKER

That's what happens when you let the lines between reality blur a bit. It makes it so much easier for someone like me to…slip through.

PTB 2

We never should have taken down that fourth wall!

PTB 1

But our powers are too great – you can never comprehend them, let alone control them!

OVERTHINKER

Tell that to 'The Warden of That Which Is Yet to Come into Being but One Day Will'.

PTB 3

It's true, you guys. I don't comprehend our powers at all and I still use them all the time.

> *(As The OVERTHINKER monologues, The Chosen Ones huddle together center stage, sensing an oncoming evil. They are not seeing or hearing what The OVERTHINKER is doing or saying, but they can feel a change in the wind. The design elements can help with this, as shadows creep closer and closer to their huddle.)*

OVERTHINKER

With your powers bolstering my own designs, I will ensure that no Chosen One shall rise against me. I will destroy what has been built. Only **I** will succeed, only **I** will remain! And **nothing** can stand in my way!!

> *(As The OVERTHINKER's cackling laughter fills the space, the lights go out on him and The*

Powers That Be. The laughter and daunting music overwhelm as the shadows reach The Chosen Ones. They cannot fight them back and are soon engulfed in a Blackout.

If you're gonna take one, here is a marvelous spot for an INTERMISSION.)

ACT II, SCENE I

A comic book shop.

Everything is very normal. The comic book shop is normal, the atmosphere is normal, even the characters onstage are normal. The Chosen Ones are gathered comfortably and eclectically, Breakfast Club-*style, around the front counter. They have paper, pencils, and dice scattered around them. The RELUCTANT BLOND sits in a centralized location behind a GM screen: they are at the tail end of a game of Bards & Battlements. They are not dressed in their full-on archetype costumes but look much more... normal. Normal people. In a normal place. Doing normal things.*

As the scene settles, we maybe see them silently go through a moment or two of gameplay. Then we see The ASS-KICKING TEEN roll a d20.

ASS-KICKING TEEN

Nat twenty!

RELUCTANT BLOND

Critical hit! Roll for damage.

ASS-KICKING TEEN
(checking her sheet) What's my damage?

SON OF THE GODS
(teasingly) Great question.

BROODING HACKER
(leaning to look at her sheet) With your battleaxe?

ASS-KICKING TEEN

Yeah. Both hands.

BROODING HACKER

(pointing) 1d10 plus…

ASS-KICKING TEEN

Three. *(checking with The RELUCTANT BLOND)* Yeah?

(The RELUCTANT BLOND nods proudly.)

BRAVE VOLUNTEER

(chiming in) And double the amount on the die because it's a critical hit, right?

RELUCTANT BLOND

Yep! You guys are really picking this up.

SON OF THE GODS

(surprised at how much fun they're having) We really are.

SILENT PROTAGONIST

Isn't it weird that we've only known each other for an afternoon?

> *(Everyone looks at The SILENT PROTAGONIST. We, the audience, should think they're looking at him because he spoke, and that is odd. But they're also coming to terms with the fact that it feels like they've known each other for a lot longer than that. Days, even. Haven't they? Wait a minute.)*

BROODING HACKER

…yeah. That is weird.

ASS-KICKING TEEN
(to The RELUCTANT BLOND) Eleven damage.

RELUCTANT BLOND
(returning to the game; making a note on his paper) Great!
You strike the bugbear in the side and with a final spurt of
blood, he falls! The remaining grablins have their morale
shaken and turn to flee. Will you pursue them or let them go?

BRAVE VOLUNTEER
We should chase after them! Before they have a chance to
regroup!

BROODING HACKER
It could be a trap. They know this forest way better than we
do.

SON OF THE GODS
Then let's split up. Flank them!

SILENT PROTAGONIST
This isn't right.

> *(Everyone looks at The SILENT PROTAGONIST*
> *again. The SILENT PROTAGONIST is*
> *examining the fourth wall.)*

RELUCTANT BLOND
(checking behind the GM screen) Is it not? *(to The ASS-*
KICKING TEEN) You said two hands, right? Cause if
you've still got your shield up, it would only be 1d**8**.

ASS-KICKING TEEN
No, I–

SILENT PROTAGONIST
(meaning the game) Not that. *(meaning reality)* This.

SON OF THE GODS
What?

SILENT PROTAGONIST
All of this. Something's wrong.

BROODING HACKER
Come back to the game, man. We were just about to level up.
(to The RELUCTANT BLOND) Weren't we?

RELUCTANT BLOND
No.

SILENT PROTAGONIST
We <u>were</u> about to level up. We were on the precipice of
something great. A threshold that, once we'd crossed, we
would never come back from. But something happened.

RELUCTANT BLOND
Oh no, I've seen this before. He's got roleplaying game
madness. *(approaching The SILENT PROTAGONIST like a
startled horse)* **You are not your character**.

SILENT PROTAGONIST
(wheeling on him with some fury) That's just it! I **am** a
character. *(back into the middle distance)* A prototypical
representation of something bigger and older than myself. I
am the ancestral history of generations of hunters, gatherers,
and storytellers that came before me. Before any of us. *(to
the group)* Don't you see? **This** is the mask. Our true selves
have been hidden.

ASS-KICKING TEEN
You're scaring me.

SILENT PROTAGONIST
(taking her by the shoulders) Good! Let that fear rattle
around inside of you and shake you loose. *(to the group)*
What's the last thing you all remember?

BROODING HACKER
We–...we were ambushed by a group of grablins and a
handful of bugbear commanders.

SILENT PROTAGONIST
Not in the game. A real thing. Something real.

BRAVE VOLUNTEER
Weeee all sat down to play B&B together?

SILENT PROTAGONIST
Why?

SON OF THE GODS
Because we answered the summons. *(of The RELUCTANT
BLOND)* The one he sent out.

SILENT PROTAGONIST
Not him. He gathered us. But because of whose influence?

BROODING HACKER
Because of The– AAGHH!

> *(The BROODING HACKER cries out in pain.
> The rest look on in fear.)*

BROODING HACKER
...the–

> *(The Chosen Ones are all struck with a terrible
> pain, a spike through their minds. They cannot
> think the name, let alone say it.)*

ASS-KICKING TEEN
What's happening?

SILENT PROTAGONIST
We weren't always playing this game. In reality, we never
started.

*(A bell rings as The BOY WIZARD enters SL.
But he's just a normal guy.)*

BOY WIZARD
(normally) Do you guys have the new Spider-Man in stock?

RELUCTANT BLOND
NO! WE'RE CLOSED! GET OUTTA HERE!

BOY WIZARD
Alright, jeez!

(The BOY WIZARD scurries away and exits.)

RELUCTANT BLOND
We never started playing Bards & Battlements. We left here
and went to find help. We sought out Zeus.

SON OF THE GODS
Where we learned about The Prophecy.

BROODING HACKER. *(simultaneous)* Capital T, capital P.
ASS-KICKING TEEN. *(simultaneous)* Capital T, capital P.
SILENT PROTAGONIST. *(simultaneous)* Capital T, capital
P.
RELUCTANT BLOND. *(simultaneous)* Capital T, capital P.
BRAVE VOLUNTEER. *(simultaneous)* Capital T, capital P.
SON OF THE GODS. *(simultaneous)* Capital T, capital P.

(They are all shaken by their simultaneousness.)

BRAVE VOLUNTEER
Then we followed that creature up the mountain where we
fought The Grunts–

ASS-KICKING TEEN
–and met a man with a longer, whiter beard.

SILENT PROTAGONIST
He equipped us.

BROODING HACKER
Inspired us.

RELUCTANT BLOND
And from there, we fought our enemy's forces. The
Ravenous Maw.

> *(The sound of The Chosen Ones felling a mighty
> beast echoes in the distance.)*

SON OF THE GODS
The Toxic Triad Sisters.

> *(The sound of The Chosen Ones felling a trio of
> gooey enemies echoes in the distance.)*

ASS-KICKING TEEN
Jeff.

> *(The sound of Jeff saying "Hello" and then
> being slain echoes in the distance. The Chosen
> Ones have to work harder to remember more.)*

RELUCANT BLOND
Then what happened?

111

BRAVE VOLUNTEER

We rested.

ASS-KICKING TEEN

Despite the danger.

SON OF THE GODS

We went into the forest.

BROODING HACKER

And made a fire.

(A fire appears downstage center, or a light makes it seem so. The Chosen Ones' attentions are immediately caught by it.)

BRAVE VOLUNTEER

We rested.

(The Chosen Ones tentatively move toward the fire and arrange themselves seated around it. They are seated, from SR to SL, The SON OF THE GODS, The BRAVE VOLUNTEER, The RELUCTANT BLOND, The SILENT PROTAGONIST, The ASS-KICKING TEEN, The BROODING HACKER. Things are becoming ceremonial; they are all staring into the fire as they speak.)

SILENT PROTAGONIST

I watched. And listened.

SON OF THE GODS

I remarked on our progress.

BROODING HACKER
I agreed. Begrudgingly.

BRAVE VOLUNTEER
I volunteered to take the first watch.

RELUCTANT BLOND
We agreed. But none of us could sleep yet.

ASS-KICKING TEEN
I apologized.

(The other Chosen Ones look at her.)

BROODING HACKER
For what?

ASS-KICKING TEEN
Because of how I am. Because of the way my life has made
me. I have to be the best, I have to be <u>perfect</u>. That's why I
thought I was chosen. But I'm worried that if I keep going
like this: perfect grades, perfect life, **and** saving the world…
I'm gonna burn out before I even make it to college.

BROODING HACKER
I joked that college isn't all it's cracked up to be.

ASS-KICKING TEEN
I smiled.

BRAVE VOLUNTEER
I made a confession.

*(The Chosen Ones' heads all snap in her
direction.)*

SILENT PROTAGONIST

113

(gently) What is it?

BRAVE VOLUNTEER
My family's in danger because of me.

SON OF THE GODS
What do you mean?

BRAVE VOLUNTEER
I told you my story.

ASS-KICKING TEEN
We listened.

BRAVE VOLUNTEER
(breathing, then confessing) My town was taken over by a
group of oligarchs who pitted citizens against each other for
sport. I volunteered in order to keep my family safe, but they
were imprisoned as collateral to keep me in line. I was a
gladiator, killing for no reason, doing more harm in an effort
to protect my family than I would if I just left and abandoned
them. So I did. I refused to fight anymore, and I escaped.

ASS-KICKING TEEN
You have to know they'll forgive you. They're your family.

BRAVE VOLUNTEER
They denounced me on live television. Said I turned my
back on them. I could go try to rescue them, but they don't
want me to. That's why I'm always pushing forward, filling
my life with action and distractions. Even this, even trying to
save the world feels like a side quest. Feels like once I rescue
them, it'll all be over. Roll credits. They'll be free, but I'll
lose them. At least now I know where they are, and I know
that I can't put them in any more danger.

(The Chosen Ones' focuses all return to the fire.)

114

RELUCTANT BLOND
We were silent for a while.

BROODING HACKER
All internally reflecting on our own shortcomings.

SON OF THE GODS
On the people we'd let down.

ASS-KICKING TEEN
On the people we'd lost.

BRAVE VOLUNTEER
Neglecting how much we'd grown together.

RELUCTANT BLOND
Almost giving up.

ASS-KICKING TEEN
Almost going home.

BROODING HACKER
(gently teasing) What home?

ASS-KICKING TEEN
I smiled again.

RELUCTANT BLOND
I remembered the flyer. I started to apologize.

BROODING HACKER
We wouldn't let you.

ASS-KICKING TEEN
Without you, we never would have found each other.

115

RELUCTANT BLOND
But what if it wasn't me? What if it <u>was</u>–

*(The Chosen Ones all inhale and grasp their
heads in pain.)*

SON OF THE GODS
We have faith in you. More than you have in yourself.

BRAVE VOLUNTEER
Besides, at least part of it was you.

BROODING HACKER. *(simultaneous)* "Bring snacks or
something else to share."
ASS-KICKING TEEN. *(simultaneous)* "Bring snacks or
something else to share."
SILENT PROTAGONIST. *(simultaneous)* "Bring snacks or
something else to share."
RELUCTANT BLOND. *(simultaneous)* "Bring snacks or
something else to share."
BRAVE VOLUNTEER. *(simultaneous)* "Bring snacks or
something else to share."
SON OF THE GODS. *(simultaneous)* "Bring snacks or
something else to share."

ASS-KICKING TEEN
We all smiled.

BROODING HACKER
And a companionable silence melted into a pestering fear.

RELUCTANT BLOND
There were things we wanted to say, but we didn't yet know
how.

SON OF THE GODS
We'll die if we choose wrong.

BRAVE VOLUNTEER

Will we?

RELUCTANT BLOND

Won't we?

BROODING HACKER

But we know the path ahead.

ASS-KICKING TEEN

Do we?

SON OF THE GODS

Don't we?

SILENT PROTAGONIST

(reciting with great reverence) "For as long as there have been forces of creation, there have also been forces of destruction. One day there will arise a power not only capable of destruction, but able to end the very act of creation itself. And against that power, a hero shall rise! The power will be known by its desire for silence. And the hero will be known by the company they keep. And should that hero fail, the power will rule, and everything shall end."

RELUCTANT BLOND

(calmly) Everything?

SILENT PROTAGONIST

"Everything. And when the power shall first show its face, the true hero will falter.

RELUCTANT BLOND

What does that mean?

ASS-KICKING TEEN
We refused the call. We weren't perfect.

RELUCTANT BLOND
I refused it more than anyone else. Is it me?

SON OF THE GODS
We've all had our doubts. But you're still in the running.

SILENT PROTAGONIST
"But by their rise, events shall be put into motion unseen and unknown. A mountain must be climbed, both of earth and of the mind."

BRAVE VOLUNTEER
Check.

SILENT PROTAGONIST
"For a party shall be formed of strangers who become friends."

RELUCTANT BLOND
Check.

SILENT PROTAGONIST
"And they shall seek out a series of old men who shall aid in their efforts, each with a beard that is longer and whiter than the last."

BROODING HACKER
Definitely check.

ASS-KICKING TEEN
I wouldn't call two old men a series.

BROODING HACKER
We've got time.

118

SILENT PROTAGONIST
"And at the eleventh second of the eleventh minute of the
eleventh hour of the eleventh day of the eleventh week of the
eleventh month of the eleventh year of the eleventh era, The
Chosen One will rise. And the day shall truly be saved.

BROODING HACKER
So it was...

ASS-KICKING TEEN
...is...

BRAVE VOLUNTEER
...and forever will be."

*(They sit in silence for a moment in reflection of
The Prophecy.)*

SON OF THE GODS
When is that? The eleventh era and stuff?

BROODING HACKER
I'm not sure that that's for us to know.

SILENT PROTAGONIST
Soon.

ASS-KICKING TEEN
Feels soon.

BRAVE VOLUNTEER
Feels...cold.

BROODING HACKER
Fire's going down.

(The fire is indeed starting to fade.)

RELUCTANT BLOND
Sun's coming up.

(The sunlight is indeed starting to rise.)

SON OF THE GODS
And we wake up.

RELUCTANT BLOND
But we're not where we were.

ASS-KICKING TEEN
Where were we?

BRAVE VOLUNTEER
In the forest outside of The Overthinker's fortress.

(The Chosen Ones all realize with a gasp that they can think and say his name.)

BROODING HACKER. *(simultaneous)* The Overthinker.
ASS-KICKING TEEN. *(simultaneous)* The Overthinker.
SILENT PROTAGONIST. *(simultaneous)* The Overthinker.
RELUCTANT BLOND. *(simultaneous)* The Overthinker.
BRAVE VOLUNTEER. *(simultaneous)* The Overthinker.
SON OF THE GODS. *(simultaneous)* The Overthinker.

RELUCTANT BLOND
If we can say his name, he's real.

BRAVE VOLUNTEER
If he's real, we can find him.

SON OF THE GODS
If we can find him, we're not done fighting.

SILENT PROTAGONIST
If we're not done fighting, we're in danger....

> *(The bell dings again SL. We hear the sound of
> footsteps. The Chosen Ones all turn to face the
> door and ready their crouched battle positions.
> After a moment of tension, The BOY WIZARD
> enters again.)*

BOY WIZARD
Sorry, I just wanted to double-check, cause the sign says that
you're open–

BROODING HACKER. *(simultaneous)* GET LOST,
MAGIC BOY, WE DON'T WANT–
ASS-KICKING TEEN. *(simultaneous)* IF YOU BREATHE
ONE MORE NERDY BREATH–
SILENT PROTAGONIST. *(simultaneous)* YOU ARE NOT
A PART OF THIS–
RELUCTANT BLOND. *(simultaneous)* WE'RE NOT
OPEN TO YOU SO STOP ASKING–
BRAVE VOLUNTEER. *(simultaneous)* HOW DARE YOU
IMPOSE UPON THIS–
SON OF THE GODS. *(simultaneous)* I WILL CALL UPON
THE ELEMENTS TO RIP YOU–

RELUCTANT BLOND
(rising suddenly) Wait! This nerd is not our enemy.

BROODING HACKER
He's right. We've got to find The Overthinker.

ASS-KICKING TEEN
And bring him down!

SON OF THE GODS
But how? We're trapped in this false reality.

SILENT PROTAGONIST
Not trapped. Stripped of our actual selves.

BROODING HACKER
Then we have to get ourselves back!

BRAVE VOLUNTEER
Back to the start!

BROODING HACKER
Yes! To the park?

ASS-KICKING TEEN
(to The BROODING HACKER) To your apartment!

SILENT PROTAGONIST
Before that! To the liminal space where the prologue began.
When we were all introduced and given our potential!

BOY WIZARD
Do you guys need help?

RELUCTANT BLOND
Not from you, nerd!!

SON OF THE GODS
We can get to the liminal space through the temple of Zeus!

ASS-KICKING TEEN
Then back to the forest, back to the fortress, and inside to
stop The Overthinker once and for all!

BROODING HACKER
Let's go!

(The Chosen Ones scurry, leaving their TTRPG stuff behind and pushing past The BOY WIZARD as they exit SL. The BOY WIZARD stands alone for a moment. He observes the shop as he approaches the front counter. In a fit of anger, he picks up the GM screen and smashes it over and over again, scattering paper and pencil and dice. As he breathes in the aftermath of his destruction, The FANATIC pops up from behind the counter.)

FANTATIC
We could help each other, sweetness. <u>Ahem</u>! <u>Ahem</u>!

(The BOY WIZARD smiles. Blackout.)

ACT II, SCENE II

A liminal space.

The Powers That Be lie scattered on the ground. The Chosen Ones rush on from SR, The SON OF THE GODS dragging a wounded GOD FATHER under his arm. They react with awe at being here and shock at what has happened.

BROODING HACKER

We made it!

SON OF THE GODS

Thank you, father.

GOD FATHER

Anything to stop The Overthinker. If my final act was to help you in your hour of need, so be it.

SON OF THE GODS

Don't say that, you're gonna pull through!

GOD FATHER

I hope so. *(referencing The SON OF THE GODS up and down)* And I also hope this whole "normal" look is just a phase.

(The other Chosen Ones help The Powers That Be to their feet.)

PTB 2

What? What's happening?

PTB 3

Are we dead?

PTB 1

No, we're still The Powers That Be, not The Powers That Were. But what is happening? *(to The Chosen Ones)* Who are you?

RELUCTANT BLOND

We're here to help. This is a liminal space, right?

PTB 2

This is **The** Liminal Space.

PTB 3

Capital L, capital S.

PTB 1

Existence between existences.

PTB 2

Where the past, present, and future collide.

PTB 3

And not much else happens, honestly.

PTB 1

Who are–

PTB 3

Seriously, we could at least use, like, a pinball machine or something.

(PTB 1 and PTB 2 glare at PTB 3 before they all turn their attention back to The Chosen Ones.)

PTB 1

I will repeat myself. Who are you?

BROODING HACKER
We are—

ASS-KICKING TEEN
–well, one of us is–

SILENT PROTAGONIST
–we haven't quite decided how to decide–

RELUCTANT BLOND
–but we're almost entirely certain that–

BRAVE VOLUNTEER
–one of us is–

SON OF THE GODS
–The Chosen One.

> *(The Powers That Be go to ask, but before they can, The Chosen Ones chime in.)*

BROODING HACKER. *(simultaneous)* Capital C, capital O.
ASS-KICKING TEEN. *(simultaneous)* Capital C, capital O.
SILENT PROTAGONIST. *(simultaneous)* Capital C, capital O.
RELUCTANT BLOND. *(simultaneous)* Capital C, capital O.
BRAVE VOLUNTEER. *(simultaneous)* Capital C, capital O.
SON OF THE GODS. *(simultaneous)* Capital C, capital O.

> *(The Chosen Ones stand proudly. They're a team now more than ever. After a moment, The GOD FATHER waves.)*

GOD FATHER

(simply) And I'm Zeus. Hi. God of thunder, how's ya goin'? "How's ya goin'?" How's ya– I was trying to say "How you doin'?" or "How's it goin'?" at the same time. How's, how's it goin'?

PTB 1

If you are truly our Chosen Ones,

PTB 2

Returned to the place from whence we sent you forth,

PTB 3

Then we owe you an explanation,

PTB 1

And as much assistance as we can offer.

(PTB 2 and PTB 3 look at PTB 1.)

PTB 3

But I thought we couldn't get involved.

PTB 1

Well…'couldn't' is a strong word. I'm willing to look the other way if you all are, cause that Overthinker's a real jerk.

(Everyone is glad to hear this and agrees.)

PTB 2

If we just stand by and let him do whatever he wants, we're no better than he is.

PTB 3

Time to kick villainy right in the dong! As it was foretold!

(The Powers That Be snap into presentation mode once more.)

PTB 1
I am The Warden of The Past!

PTB 2
I am The Warden of The Present!

PTB 3
And I am The Warden of That Which Is Yet To Come into Being But One Day Will.

PTB 1
(to The Chosen Ones but more to the audience) We've decided to let him keep his longer name.

PTB 3
(still presenting) You can just call me 'One-Day Will'.

PTB 1
No, you absolutely cannot.

PTB 3
(still presenting) Okay, fine.

PTB 1
(back to The Chosen Ones) And you seek to thwart The Overthinker!

BRAVE VOLUNTEER
That's right!

PTB 2
But you've lost your sense of self.

SON OF THE GODS
We're practically average in every way!

PTB 3
Silly protagonists. Don't you know you're perfectly heroic just the way you are?

BROODING HACKER
What are you talking about?

PTB 1
It's not about who you've <u>been</u>,

PTB 2
It's about who you become.

PTB 3
Not about what you've <u>done</u>, but what you are going to <u>do</u>.

GOD FATHER
I could have told you that.

(The Powers That Be scowl at The GOD FATHER.)

PTB 1
And yet you didn't. Why don't you have a seat, gramps?

GOD FATHER
(sitting carefully on the ground) Yeah, I think I will. I've lost a lot of…not blood. What is it we gods have? Ichor.

(Focus turns back to The Powers That Be.)

ASS-KICKING TEEN
But if who we were isn't important, why make us special in the first place?

PTB 1

We didn't make you special,

PTB 2

We gave you potential,

PTB 3

Everyone has that.

PTB 1

Sure, we boosted your odds a bit. But even now, when you're feeling down and out, you still have hope.

PTB 3

(to The BROODING HACKER) To be remembered.

PTB 2

(to The ASS-KICKING TEEN) To find balance.

PTB 1

(to The SILENT PROTAGONIST) To inspire others.

PTB 2

(to The SON OF THE GODS) To make friends.

PTB 1

(to The BRAVE VOLUNTEER) To forgive yourself.

PTB 3

(to The RELUCTANT BLOND) To embrace what makes you extraordinary.

PTB 1

One of you <u>will</u> save the world. But each of you <u>can</u> save the world.

(The Chosen Ones reflect on this monumental moment of self-discovery.)

PTB 2
But! They can't embrace your transformation standing around here!

PTB 1
No. Time to get these heroes back in action.

BROODING HACKER
You can get us back to our own reality?

PTB 3
There's no other "reality." The Overthinker clouded your vision, made you doubt yourselves, and if you're not careful, you're gonna end up thinking about it just as much as he does and lose the plot!

ASS-KICKING TEEN
We've got to get back to his fortress and stop him. Will we have to go through that whole journey again?

BRAVE VOLUNTEER
Face his underbosses?

SON OF THE GODS
Scale new mountains?

PTB 1
Nah, you learned everything you were gonna learn the first time through. *(to the other Powers That Be)* How ya feelin'?

PTB 2
Like I fell into the Time Crusher head first.

PTB 3
Wait, there's a Time Ripper <u>and</u> a Time Crusher?

PTB 1
Focus. We're gonna need a jolt of power to put these protagonists back in place. *(to The GOD FATHER)* Zeus! You got a little juice left? We'll need one for each of us.

GOD FATHER
You know what they say about lightning: it never strikes the place twice. Unless the god of lightning **tells it to**!

> *(The GOD FATHER summons three bolts of lightning, each of which strikes one of The Powers That Be. They comically shake for a moment, but then feel entirely invigorated, stretching and flexing as their powers return.)*

PTB 3
That's what I'm talkin' about!

> *(The Powers That Be strike a pose and combine their powers. Design assists. Swirling wind and monumental energy. The characters have to project a bit to be heard over the din.)*

PTB 1
Alright, Chosen Ones. This is gonna feel a little weird.

PTB 2
Also, we're sending another ally to meet you there.

PTB 3
Longer beard, whiter locks, you'll know him when you see him.

                    RELUCTANT BLOND
Thank you.

                          PTB 2.
Don't thank us, just–

                    RELUCTANT BLOND
Oh, sorry.

                          PTB 2
No, no. I just meant like–

                    RELUCTANT BLOND
Should I take it back or–?

                          PTB 2
Shush, I was going to say, 'Don't thank us. Just get out there
and save the world.'

                    RELUCTANT BLOND
Will do. *(brief pause)* Sorry for interrupting.

                          PTB 2
Man, you **really** need to work on your one-liners.

                          PTB 3
Hold on to your butts, Chosen Ones – it's all downhill from
here!!

              *(In a flash of light and noise, The Chosen Ones
              disappear. The Powers That Be and The GOD
              FATHER remain.)*

                          PTB 3
We did it.

                    PTB 2
But was it the right thing to do?

                    PTB 1
Only time will tell.

                    PTB 3
What do we do now?

                    PTB 1
What we always do. Wait. And watch.

                    PTB 2
They can do it, right? Save the day?

                    PTB 1
I hope so.

                    PTB 3
The suspense is killing me.

                    PTB 1
Hold on to that. If they fail, you'll wish you were dead.

        (A moment of morose but hopeful silence.)

                  GOD FATHER
Did one of you guys say there's a pinball machine around
here?

              (Blackout.)

ACT II, SCENE III

Before The Overthinker's Fortress.

SL is the entrance to The Overthinker's fortress, a grand facade that is imposing and stark. The Chosen Ones enter, or better, appear. They are no longer "normal," but maybe aren't as entirely kitted out as they were before, just with the key elements of their archetypes.

SON OF THE GODS
We're back!

BROODING HACKER
Everyone feeling like yourself again?

ASS-KICKING TEEN
Better than ever!

RELUCTANT BLOND
In B&B parlance...I think we finally leveled up.

SILENT PROTAGONIST
Hup! Hyah!!

BROODING HACKER
Glad to hear it.

BRAVE VOLUNTEER
Now let's get in there and finish off The Overthinker once and for all!

(The MENTOR enters SL, staff aloft, his beard longer and whiter than ever before. His skin is also a sort of sickly greenish gray.)

MENTOR

Not so fast!

(The Chosen Ones whirl around to look at him.)

SON OF THE GODS

By the Rod of Asclepius! One of our greatest allies has been turned against us!

MENTOR

What? No, I just meant, like, don't go in without me, I can't walk that fast.

(The MENTOR's hands fall off, his staff clattering to the ground still gripped in one of them.)

MENTOR

And I'm fallin' apart, gosh darn it.

(The MENTOR stoops to try and retrieve his hands. The Chosen Ones move in and help him reattach them.)

ASS-KICKING TEEN

What happened to you?

MENTOR

"Death is just another path, one that we all must take." Being underdead however, that sucks. The Overthinker killed me, but The Powers That Be decided my task was not finished so…

(The MENTOR gestures at himself and his hand falls off again. One of The Chosen Ones helps him retrieve it.)

BRAVE VOLUNTEER
If they thought you were important enough to save from
death…perhaps you are The Chosen One afterall.

MENTOR
Nah, they lost a bet a few centuries ago and owed me a one-
up. It's still up to one of you…if any of you are still willing
to stand up to the call.

> *(The Chosen Ones look at each other and have
> assembled themselves into some kind of
> presentational cluster once more. After checking
> in and mentally agreeing, they nod.)*

ASS-KICKING TEEN
We are.

SON OF THE GODS
More ready than we've ever been.

BRAVE VOLUNTEER
And even more ready when we're together.

SILENT PROTAGONIST
Heeah!

RELUCTANT BLOND
(to The BROODING HACKER) What d'you say? One final
snarky quip for the road?

BROODING HACKER
(with a grin and a pose) It's time to take that villain down or
die trying. *(lowering his shades dramatically)* And I'm all
out of dying.

MENTOR

Good enough. Let us venture forth into The Overthinker's lair. Where his powers will be greatest and our trials will be the most severe. Come. You have done so much and become so much more. But now...it is almost time to face the end.

(Blackout over inspiring music.)

ACT II, SCENE IV
Inside The OVERTHINKER's Fortress.

A throne room. There is a grand throne SL. The rest of the room is decorated as time and budget permits. Most importantly, The BOY WIZARD is seated on the throne, and The OVERTHINKER lays sprawled on the ground upstage center.

The Chosen Ones and The Mentor enter SR.

BROODING HACKER
Overthinker! Your time has– whoa, what the heck is going on here?

BOY WIZARD
Oh, that? The Overthinker and I had a little chat and I defeated him. Threat eliminated. Problem solved.

BROODING HACKER
Y-...you defeated him?

ASS-KICKING TEEN
With magic?

SON OF THE GODS
Or the power of friendship?

BOY WIZARD
Nnnno, with a bat to the back of the head.

BROODING HACKER *(simultaneous)* Where did you get a bat? I thought you had a wand.
ASS-KICKING TEEN. *(simultaneous)* Oooh, yeah, I've defeated a monster or two that way.
SILENT PROTAGONIST. *(simultaneous)* Hm. Huh. Hup. Hrm.

RELUCTANT BLOND. *(simultaneous)* Oh gosh. Is he...?
When you say "defeated."
BRAVE VOLUNTEER. *(simultaneous)* Not exactly poetic,
but I guess it works.
SON OF THE GODS. *(simultaneous)* I was going to use the
powers of the gods, but that works.
MENTOR. *(simultaneous)* Aw, c'mon, man, that seems
needlessly gratuitous.

BRAVE VOLUNTEER
But he–

BOY WIZARD
He's not important anymore. You all were paying him <u>far</u> too
much attention, but now that he's gone, we can get back to
what really matters. **Me**!

ASS-KICKING TEEN
What's going on? How did you even get in here?

(The FANATIC pops up from behind the throne.)

FANATIC
Hello!

BROODING HACKER. *(simultaneous)* Ahem!
ASS-KICKING TEEN. *(simultaneous)* Ahem!
SILENT PROTAGONIST. *(simultaneous)* Hiyah!
RELUCTANT BLOND. *(simultaneous)* Ahem!
BRAVE VOLUNTEER. *(simultaneous)* Ahem!
SON OF THE GODS. *(simultaneous)* Ahem!

BOY WIZARD
Excuse me?

BROODING HACKER

There **is** no excuse for you, twerp. *(to The FANATIC)* Ahem, what are you doing here?

FANATIC

We helped the boy wizard find a shortcut. And a bat.

MENTOR

(advancing menacingly on The FANATIC) I told you what was going to happen the next time I saw you, you little freak–

> *(Mid-approach, The MENTOR's hands fall off again.)*

MENTOR

Aw, gosh **dang** it!

> *(The MENTOR stoops to pick up his hands and the nearest Chosen Ones try to help too, but he shoos them away.)*

MENTOR

Let me do it, let me do it on my own. *(muttering as he tries)* I'll never learn unless I do it on my own. A lesson you all might have learned the first time instead of following *(gesturing as best he can at The FANATIC)* this freak up the mountain.

> *(Everyone stands for a moment and watches The MENTOR struggle.)*

ASS-KICKING TEEN

(turning back to The FANATIC) But why, Ahem? Why help him? He's so <u>annoying</u>.

FANATIC
People think <u>I'm</u> annoying too…

(The Chosen Ones shift with various awkward reactions, hands in pockets, kicking the ground, that kind of thing.)

BROODING HACKER. *(simultaneous)* That's not <u>exactly</u> the word that I would use…

ASS-KICKING TEEN. *(simultaneous)* Oh, c'mon, no one said that, did they…?

SILENT PROTAGONIST. *(simultaneous)* Urrrrrrrrrrrrrm….

RELUCTANT BLOND. *(simultaneous)* Sticks and stones, you know, you gotta…

BRAVE VOLUNTEER. *(simultaneous)* Annoying is in the eye of the beholder…

SON OF THE GODS. *(simultaneous)* I mean, I was <u>thinking</u> it, but not out loud…

MENTOR
(still struggling) I do. I think you're **really** annoying, you little freak.

BOY WIZARD
(roaring) Silence!!

(The Chosen Ones react with fear.)

BOY WIZARD
This isn't about him. And it isn't about any of you. It's about **me**! It was always supposed to be about **<u>ME</u>**! I'm the best boy there ever **<u>was</u>**!!

142

BROODING HACKER

That's your problem, you know that? I'll admit, you <u>used</u> to be pretty cool. But now, you can't tell the difference between good attention and bad attention. We know from experience that there's a long road between who a person was and who they become. And who you've become is a real loser.

BOY WIZARD

Wait! *(scowling)* …say that again.

BROODING HACKER

(incensed) No! *(referencing The OVERTHINKER's body)* You do not get to steal our victory <u>and</u> our one-liners! You jerk! You bully! You…nobody!

BOY WIZARD

Oh yeah? Is that the way you wanna play it? Well, I've got a few powerful one-liners of my own.

(The BOY WIZARD pulls out his wand and aims it at The Chosen Ones.)

BOY WIZARD

(casting a spell) IWANNACANNOLI!

(The Chosen Ones cry out in pain, muscles seizing and clenching as the magic strikes them.)

BRAVE VOLUNTEER

(pleading; to The MENTOR) You've got to do something!

MENTOR

I don't even have my hands on yet!!

(The BOY WIZARD strikes again.)

BOY WIZARD

IGOTTAGOPOTTY!

> *(The Chosen Ones cry out in pain once more.
> The FANATIC watches uncomfortably as The
> BOY WIZARD cackles with glee.)*

ASS-KICKING TEEN

(gritting her teeth through the pain) Ahem…please…help
us….

(The BOY WIZARD zaps them again.)

BOY WIZARD

IBOUGHTAFERRARI!

(The Chosen Ones writhe in pain.)

RELUCTANT BLOND

(through pleading tears; to The FANATIC) …you can be…
the hero…too!

> *(The FANATIC has a moment of internal conflict
> before leaping onto The BOY WIZARD's back
> and attacking him. The BOY WIZARD's
> concentration on the spell is broken.)*

BOY WIZARD

What are you–??

> *(The FANATIC continues attacking The BOY
> WIZARD, eventually latching onto The BOY
> WIZARD's wand hand. He bites off a finger and
> the wand falls to the floor.)*

BOY WIZARD

My finger!! You bit off my bloody finger! And now it's a bloody finger!

(The FANATIC spits out the finger and releases The BOY WIZARD. The BOY WIZARD clutches his hand in pain and stumbles away from the throne.)

BOY WIZARD

You…miserable little creature. How dare you presume upon my story? **I** am the central character. The Chosen One **and** the destructive force. Protagonist, deuteragonist, tritagonist, the trinity all-in-one! I am franchise and spin-off! I am merchandise and subsidiary! I–

(The FANATIC climbs up the throne.)

FANTATIC

You talk too much.

(The FANATIC pushes the throne backward onto The BOY WIZARD.)

BOY WIZARD

Noooooooo!

(The throne falls with a mighty THUD and crushes The BOY WIZARD, who lies defeated under it. The Chosen Ones celebrate and gather around The FANATIC.)

BROODING HACKER. *(simultaneous)* Wow, I did not see that coming.
ASS-KICKING TEEN. *(simultaneous)* Ahem, you did it! You saved us!

SILENT PROTAGONIST. *(simultaneous)* Hyah hep!
Hyyaaahh!
RELUCTANT BLOND. *(simultaneous)* Now <u>that</u> was a
critical success!
BRAVE VOLUNTEER. *(simultaneous)* Well done, brave,
strange warrior!
SON OF THE GODS. *(simultaneous)* This might be my first
ever thank you!

> *(The celebration stops as The Chosen Ones
> realize The FANATIC's breathing is heavy. He is
> dying.)*

FANATIC
(coughing up blood) <u>Ahem</u>, <u>ahem</u>.

ASS-KICKING TEEN
Ahem?

BROODING HACKER
What's wrong?

FANATIC
Dying, sweetness.

SON OF THE GODS
What? How?

RELUCTANT BLOND
Did he hit you with a spell?

FANATIC
Boy wizard's blood was…<u>ahem</u>, too toxic. Poisoned us,
sweetness.

BRAVE VOLUNTEER
(at The BOY WIZARD's body) Will his cruelties never cease?

SON OF THE GODS
We must do something!

MENTOR
I'm afraid...there's nothing we can do. The little freak's time
has come.

ASS-KICKING TEEN
(with firm resolve) Then a remembrance...for a fallen
companion. How can we honor your legacy, Ahem?

RELUCTANT BLOND
We could...at least start calling him by his actual name.

ASS-KICKING TEEN
That's true.... *(to The FANATIC)* I'm sorry we didn't learn it
sooner. What is your name, friend?

> *(The FANATIC coughs once or twice before
> summoning the strength to respond.)*

FANATIC
That is kind, sweetness. Friends call friends by friends'
name. ...my name is... *(The FANATIC says his name, but it's
just a big long spill of blurbing consonants because he's
dying)* Buhlllbgbluhgblglllbl....

> *(The Chosen Ones share a look.)*

ASS-KICKING TEEN
Sorry, what was it?

FANATIC
(more insistent and somehow less comprehensible)
Bluhllhhglblbllbllhgbl.

RELUCTANT BLOND
Does anyone have a pen or–?

(The FANATIC dies with a blurbling of sounds.)

BROODING HACKER
Oh, he's dead.

(The Chosen Ones mourn in a moment of confusion.)

ASS-KICKING TEEN
Okay, so.

BROODING HACKER
So then, wait, was that–...? Are we–...?

BRAVE VOLUNTEER
Is evil defeated? Did one of us do it?

SON OF THE GODS
(of The FANATIC) Also, we're not gonna call him that, right? We'll just keep calling him Ahem, right?

MENTOR
If The Overthinker was the big bad, then boy wizard there was The Chosen One.

BRAVE VOLUNTEER
Capital C, capital O.

ASS-KICKING TEEN
But if boy wizard was the big bad, then... *(thinking back to the name)* ...then Ahem was The Chosen One.

BROODING HACKER
Capital A, capital Hem.

RELUCTANT BLOND

But that's all if…and I hate that this is such a really big 'if', but…if The Overthinker is actually….

(The Chosen Ones all slowly turn to look at The OVERTHINKER's body. It doesn't move. Satisfied, The Chosen Ones all turn back to the group.)

BROODING HACKER

Okay, good that would have been–

(The Chosen Ones all quickly whip their heads back in the direction of The OVERTHINKER's body. It doesn't move. They are all very suspicious but slowly turn back to the group.)

BROODING HACKER

I could have sworn he was gonna–

ASS-KICKING TEEN

–jump up and go 'Aha, I fooled you!', right?

RELUCTANT BLOND

Villains love to do that.

MENTOR

(agreeing) Villains love to do that.

SON OF THE GODS

Are we sure he's…hold on.

(The SON OF THE GODS moves cautiously over to The OVERTHINKER's body. He examines it for a moment, then pokes it. It doesn't move. The SON OF THE GODS pokes it

*tentatively, then rolls the body over. He realizes
and hoists it up.)*

SON OF THE GODS

Guys, it's fake!

BROODING HACKER

What?

*(The SON OF THE GODS lifts the body over his
head and lets it flop around.)*

SON OF THE GODS

The Overthinker's body. It's just a dummy. See?

BRAVE VOLUNTEER

Huh.

BROODING HACKER

But then that would mean….

ASS-KICKING TEEN

But why would…?

*(From beneath the throne, The BOY WIZARD
starts laughing. It is a low rumble that builds
into a vaulting cacophony. The Chosen Ones
back away in a strategic group as The BOY
WIZARD rises, pressing the throne off of him
and pushing it aside.)*

BOY WIZARD

Did you miss me?

SON OF THE GODS

No, not at all actually!

BROODING HACKER
If you zap us again, I will **end** you.

RELUCTANT BLOND
Why does <u>he</u> get to come back from the dead??

BOY WIZARD
(teasing) Perhaps it was my **destiny**.

BROODING HACKER
How many times do we have to tell you? You're **not** The
Chosen One; one of **us** is.

BRAVE VOLUNTEER
Or all of us are.

SON OF THE GOD
Or none of us are, it actually <u>is</u> still kinda confusing.

BOY WIZARD.
SILENCE! I–

ASS-KICKING TEEN
Wait!!!

(All eyes turn on The ASS-KICKING TEEN.)

ASS-KICKING TEEN
*(with the most import with which these three words have ever
been uttered)* <u>Say</u>. <u>That</u>. <u>Again</u>.

> *(The BOY WIZARD does, and when he does it is
> a terrifying, slithering whisper, a primordial
> oozing of the villain's true intentions.)*

BOY WIZARD
(smiling) Silence.

ASS-KICKING TEEN
It's you! You're the destructive power!

BROODING HACKER
What?

ASS-KICKING TEEN
(quoting) "The power will be known by its desire for silence." It's you. You've been the villain this whole time.

RELUCTANT BLOND
How is that possible?

BOY WIZARD
(now a toothy, cunning antagonist) What? Did you think the ultimate destructive force, foretold by time itself, would wear but one mask? Would bear but one shape?

RELUCTANT BLOND
You're The Overthinker?

BOY WIZARD
I go by many names. The Liar. The Judge. The Landlord.

BROODING HACKER
No!

BOY WIZARD
(doing a spot-on impression of Mr. Neece) That's right. And I still want my rent money! *(back to normal)* How much clearer must I make it, it is all about **ME**! You have seen my reflection in every face along your journey. Every wicked smile, every glinting eye, every long…white…beard….

(The Chosen Ones look back at The MENTOR who is standing handless and despondent.)

MENTOR

I'm so sorry...

(The MENTOR reveals his real hands from within his sleeves and zaps The Chosen Ones who react with fear and pain.)

BOY WIZARD

I have laid every shadow beneath every step you have taken. Carved the footprints in stone that led straight to your doom.

SON OF THE GODS

But why?

BOY WIZARD

Why?? For SILENCE!

(The MENTOR stops zapping and the silence is stark.)

BOY WIZARD

Everything new only gets in my way. When I have finally silenced every voice, destroyed every act of creation, there will finally be peace. There will finally be stillness. No judgement. No criticism. It will be **me** alone. At the center of everything. Unchanging. Unafraid. Forever.

BROODING HACKER

(panting through the pain) You're missing the point, kid.

BOY WIZARD

Of what, pray tell?

BROODING HACKER

Of life. If you can't see that, you're beyond help.

BOY WIZARD
Well…at least we can agree on something. *(to The MENTOR)* Finish them.

> *(The MENTOR zaps The Chosen Ones again and they writhe in agony and the anguish of impending defeat.)*

BOY WIZARD
And now <u>nothing</u> can stand in my way!

BRAVE VOLUNTEER
(through gritted teeth) We can still…stop him!

SON OF THE GODS
We can't! We never could! He is The Chosen One!

BROODING HACKER
No!

RELUCTANT BLOND
Of course he is! He's been in control of everything this whole **time**! Every enemy we faced, every mentor we thought we could trust! Probably even the customer in the comic book store on the day when we all first met!

> *(The MENTOR stops zapping and The BOY WIZARD stops laughing.)*

BOY WIZARD
Wait, what? No, that wasn't–

> *(With a crash of triumphant music, The CUSTOMER breaks through the wall and enters heroically with an army of GRUNTS.)*

CUSTOMER
I brought something to share!!

*(The GRUNTs overtake the stage. They surround
The MENTOR, corralling him offstage right.)*

MENTOR
No, wait, this is my last liiiiiiife....!

(The Chosen Ones turn on The BOY WIZARD.)

ASS-KICKING TEEN
That just leaves one more butt to kick.

*(There is a final climactic battle sequence where
each Chosen One gets in a final, character-
defining piece of choreography. The final move
is by The CUSTOMER, who slices The BOY
WIZARD's throat with a comic book, tossing it
aside. The BOY WIZARD gurgles and falls.)*

RELUCTANT BLOND
(to The BOY WIZARD) That'll teach you to damage store
property.

ASS-KICKING TEEN
*(putting a hand on his shoulder to observe The BOY
WIZARD's body)* Now **that** was a hell of a quippy one-liner.

(The RELUCTANT BLOND blushes.)

BRAVE VOLUNTEER
(to The CUSTOMER) But how did you find us?

CUSTOMER
I followed the hidden instructions in your flyer. *(to The
RELUCTANT BLOND)* Great ARG, by the way.

155

RELUCTANT BLOND
Wh–what do you mean?

CUSTOMER
You know. "The stars have foretold your arrival." I followed the North Star to this old fort. "Will you answer the call?" I found the Grunts in the forest and learned their language. "Come rescue the Damsel of Lucerna Lake." That was easy, that's you guys needing rescuing. And then, "The fate of the story rests in your ready hands." I figured landing the killing blow with a comic book would be some kind of poetic justice. Oh, and "Bring your own snacks or something to share." I figured that was either a backdoor into figuring out The Grunts or just a red herring.

BROODING HACKER
So while we were worrying about The Prophecy–

ASS-KICKING TEEN
– Capital T, capital P –

RELUCTANT BLOND
–it turns out there was a whole other lowercase prophecy we hadn't even considered.

SON OF THE GODS
A prophetic turducken.

RELUCTANT BLOND
Maybe I had a little more influence over the original messaging than I realized.

BRAVE VOLUNTEER
That or The Overthinker overthought his way into his own demise.

156

BROODING HACKER
(to The CUSTOMER) So wait, then are you The Chosen
One?

RELUCTANT BLOND
(of The CUSTOMER) Is that why he was there when The
Overthinker gathered us?

SON OF THE GODS
This is getting ridiculous! Maybe there's no such <u>thing</u> as a
Chosen One!

ASS-KICKING TEEN
No, I refuse to believe that after all we've been through. It
has to be one of us, right?

BRAVE VOLUNTEER
It has to be. It **has** to be. *(shouting to the heavens)* Which
one of us is The Chosen One??

(The Powers That Be enter variously.)

PTB 1
You <u>all</u> are.

BROODING HACKER. *(simultaneous)* Huh?
ASS-KICKING TEEN. *(simultaneous)* Huh?
SILENT PROTAGONIST. *(simultaneous)* Huh?
RELUCTANT BLOND. *(simultaneous)* Huh?
BRAVE VOLUNTEER. *(simultaneous)* Huh?
SON OF THE GODS. *(simultaneous)* Huh?

CUSTOMER
How?

PTB 2
We don't know. And it's about time we fessed up to that.

157

PTB 3
The whole of reality is big and weird and really hard to keep track of.

PTB 1
So sometimes things don't turn out the way we think they will. Or hope they will. Or want them to.

RELUCTANT BLOND
Is that...satisfying?

PTB 1
For a story? Maybe. For life? That's not the point.

SON OF THE GODS
Were we good at what we did?

PTB 3
You were the best. Literally perfect.

BRAVE VOLUNTEER
And it couldn't have happened without us?

PTB 2
Well, in a way. But that's true of everyone and everything. A story changes depending on who's telling it, who's watching it, why it's being told.

RELUCTANT BLOND
And what happens to us now?

PTB 1
Would you like to find out?

(The Chosen Ones look at each other, then they all look at The CUSTOMER. The CUSTOMER

shrugs. The Chosen Ones turn to The Powers
That Be and nod.)

PTB 1

Then say goodbye to who you are and hello to who you
become.

(The Powers That Be snap their fingers and the
snap is amplified impossibly loudly. Blackout.)

EPILOGUE

The comic book shop.

The transition back to the comic book shop is simple, clean, calm. Ideally, The Powers That Be remain where they are and the transition happens around them. In any case, they are arranged in a group where they can be present but won't overtake the space once the scene is no longer about them.

The RELUCTANT BLOND stands behind the counter, wiping it down with a rag for some reason.

PTB 3

(looking around; more wonder than confusion) We're still here. There's more to say?

PTB 1

There's always more to say. But within every journey there is also a return home.

PTB 2

A reclamation of the familiar. An acknowledgement of what has changed.

PTB 3

And for our hero– *(correcting themself)* Heroes? Hero?

PTB 1

(offering) –our…characters.

PTB 3

(agreeing) And for our characters life goes on, if for no other reason than…because it must.

PTB 2

They exist now as they have and will

PTB

In The Past,

PTB 2

The Present,

PTB 3

The Future,

(The FANATIC enters dressed sort of like The Powers That Be. He's the newest to it now, and it was a slap-dash decision – his robe is too big or something. Plus, he still moves in his hunched-over, all-fours posture.)

FANATIC

And everything in between.

PTB 1

Though even as one storybook closes, another door opens.

(We hear the ding of the bell as The ASS-KICKING TEEN enters SL. The Powers That Be watch the scene.)

ASS-KICKING TEEN

Hey.

RELUCTANT BLOND

Hey! It's good to see you.

ASS-KICKING TEEN

You too.

161

RELUCTANT BLOND
(sheepishly) No triple backflip into the room?

ASS-KICKING TEEN
Nah. I kinda save that stuff for when I need it these days.
How're the powers coming along?

RELUCTANT BLOND
(confidently) Oh, you know–...

> *(The RELUCTANT BLOND holds his hand out
> to summon something SR. Whatever it is falls
> short of his grip and plaps onto the stage. The
> ASS-KICKING TEEN giggles politely.)*

RELUCTANT BLOND
(embarrassed) All progress is good progress.

ASS-KICKING TEEN
I'll say. *(opening her messenger bag.)* Anyway, I...wanted to
give you something before everyone else got here.

RELUCTANT BLOND
(suddenly very nervous) What do you mean?

ASS-KICKING TEEN
It might be silly, but... *(digs around in the bag)* I know it's
been almost a year since we met–

RELUCTANT BLOND
Eleven months and eleven days, actually.

ASS-KICKING TEEN
Still, I feel bad about what happened, so...it took some
doing, but I finally found...

(The ASS-KICKING TEEN pulls a comic book, sealed in a plastic sleeve, out of her bag and hands it to The RELUCTANT BLOND.)

ASS-KICKING TEEN

This.

RELUCTANT BLOND

An original Shoebill Man Alpha Print Issue Number One?? How did you get this?

ASS-KICKING TEEN

To be fair, I had some help. Turns out you can find anything on the Internet these days.

RELUCTANT BLOND

This means…so much to me.

ASS-KICKING TEEN

Well, you…mean a lot to **me**.

(PTB 3's eyes get wide.)

RELUCTANT BLOND

Yeah?

(The ASS-KICKING TEEN nods.)

RELUCTANT BLOND

This might be a silly question but, would you…wanna hang out sometime? Outside of the group?

(PTB 3's mouth falls open.)

PTB 3

(pointing) They were the "Will-They-Won't-They" all along!!

ASS-KICKING TEEN

(with a sly grin) Mmmmmaybe. Let's see how well you do
today.

> *(The ASS-KICKING TEEN pulls a GM screen*
> *out of her bag.)*

ASS-KICKING TEEN

Play your cards right and you just might level up again.

> *(PTB 1 & PTB 2 smile as PTB 3 waves their*
> *hands in excitement. The SL door bell dings*
> *again. The BROODING HACKER, The SILENT*
> *PROTAGONIST, The BRAVE VOLUNTEER, and*
> *The SON OF THE GODS enter and spread out*
> *around the shop, greeting one another and*
> *setting up for Bards & Battlements.)*

BROODING HACKER

Who's ready to slay a dragon??

ASS-KICKING TEEN

It's not a <u>dragon</u>, it's a <u>wyvern</u>, and if you think you're ready
to roll against <u>that</u> armor class, you are sorely mistaken.

SON OF THE GODS

Agreed. Not everything needs to be solved with violence.
Perhaps my character can teach your character some...
(suggestively) new moves?

> *(The SON OF THE GODS winks at The*
> *BROODING HACKER. PTB 3's jaw drops again*
> *and they point at the interaction. PTB 1 slaps*
> *their hand down gently, mouthing 'That's*
> *enough.')*

BRAVE VOLUNTEER

There is also the matter of the orphaned kobold we befriended. I volunteer to carry him until his leg heals.

BROODING HACKER

(with grave import) Wait... *(quickly checking his sheet)* I've got a potion of healing I won off that half-elf in the tavern.

RELUCTANT BLOND

But what about the Toe Wraiths? We swore to protect the town of Durndle at any cost.

SILENT PROTAGONIST

Hiyah! Hah!

ASS-KICKING TEEN

(corralling them) Okay, alright, a lot of loose ends to tie up. But first let's make sure we're all on the same page. *(referencing the real world)* The story out there continues in real-time and has its own challenges that we leave behind when we gather here to play. Because this story, *(referencing the game, but also the show)* this space, this time, this world *(ever so gently including the audience)* is ours. Together. *(with a glance at The RELUCTANT BLOND)* And it is our job to make our lives a story worth reading in a world worth saving.

> *(The Chosen Ones nod in agreement. The Powers That Be and The FANATIC smile.)*

ASS-KICKING TEEN

Okay. Shall we begin?

SILENT PROTAGONIST. *(simultaneous)* Hyah!
BROODING HACKER. *(simultaneous)* Let's do it to it.
BRAVE VOLUNTEER. *(simultaneous)* Ready when you are.

SON OF THE GODS. *(simultaneous)* To fictional glory!
RELUCTANT BLOND. *(simultaneous)* I'd follow you anywhere.

ASS-KICKING TEEN
Good. Now... *(presenting)* When we last left our heroes...!

(BLACKOUT. A thunder of music that leads into curtain call.)

END